Industrial Revolution

A Captivating Guide to the Age of Reason

(The History and Legacy of the Rapid Scientific and Technological Advancements)

Henry McDonagh

I0558248

Published By **Phil Dawson**

Henry McDonagh

Industrial Revolution: A Captivating Guide to the Age of Reason (The History and Legacy of the Rapid Scientific and Technological Advancements)

ISBN   978-1-990373-89-3

No part of this guidebook shall be reproduced in any form without permission in writing from the publisher except in the case of brief quotations embodied in critical articles or reviews.

Legal & Disclaimer

The information contained in this book is not designed to replace or take the place of any form of medicine or professional medical advice. The information in this book has been provided for educational & entertainment purposes only.

The information contained in this book has been compiled from sources deemed reliable, and it is accurate to the best of the Author's knowledge; however, the Author cannot guarantee its accuracy and validity and cannot be held liable for any errors or omissions. Changes are periodically made to this book. You must consult your doctor or get professional medical advice before using any of the suggested remedies, techniques, or information in this book.

Upon using the information contained in this book, you agree to hold harmless the Author from and against any damages, costs, and expenses, including any legal fees potentially resulting from the application of any of the information provided by this guide. This disclaimer applies to any damages or injury caused by the use and application, whether directly or indirectly, of any advice or information presented, whether for breach of contract, tort, negligence, personal injury, criminal intent, or under any other cause of action.

You agree to accept all risks of using the information presented inside this book. You need to consult a professional medical practitioner in order to ensure you are both able and healthy enough to participate in this program.

Table Of Contents

Chapter 1: The Perfect Stage For A Revolution

"To me, there has never been a higher source of earthly honor or distinction than that connected with the advances of science." Sir Isaac Newton

William Lee was a young smart, intelligent and religious man who was from Calverton from Nottinghamshire. He attended St. John's College, and eventually, an exemplary man from the Holy cloth. However, to the delight of his friends especially his wife the gentleman was equally innovative as he was religious. In a time when man could only do things that were physically within his grasp and he was extremely beneficial advantage.

The harsh and dry terrain in the village was not anything to boast about Many of the people of the village opted to claim the rich land of the close Sherwood Forest.

A lot of them were self-employed, as shearers, becoming the primary industry in the middle ages of Nottinghamshire. They were wanted for their valuable product they carried behind their backs - the valued wool. The soft, luxurious goodness resulted in the animal's discomfort. It was alleviated through annual shearing sessions that created a win-win for the shepherds and their flocks. Wool from sheep from Nottinghamshire is renowned for its unique length as well as its rough but sturdy fibrous strands, were predominantly used for the production of an expensive form of hand-knit yarn. The delicately knitted pieces of clothing were then filled, which was a process of sanitation that saw the designers smashing on the cloth using wooden hammers within barrels stuffed with water and clay.

In 1589, the 26-year-old Lee bought a business in knitting. The company soon hired a beautiful young lady, and immediately was captivated. She was an excellent knitter who took her work very seriously. She would often decline Lee's advances due to her busy schedule, filled by the many obligations of her occupation. With the intention of speeding the process of her work so that the time she spent with her loved ones could be devoted to him, Lee invented what was also known as"the "stocking frame," all to have his lovely girlfriend for his own.

John Beniston's image of a frame for a stocking

The initial prototype was the size of a wooden piece that looked like a piano of kind, and was equipped with an armchair. Instead of black and white keys, the device "imitated the movements of hand-knitters," however it could increase the speed of knitting thanks to its eight needles.

While the frame was impressive, as beautiful as it had been, it was only able to make coarse fabric that was quite rough on the skin. But, satisfied by his invention, Lee traveled to London and pleaded with the Queen Elizabeth I to grant patents, however, his application was quickly rejected by the queen who pointed out at the abrasiveness of the fabric as well as the threat it could pose for the hand-knitting business.

Queen Elizabeth I

Although disappointed but not discouraged, the holy man spent the next several years reworking the frame and including another dozen needles to create a total of 20. In addition, nine years after the denial of his patent the new frame could now be able to handle an array of different materials, from rough, locally-grown wool to silky fabrics that were as smooth as silk. The frame was satisfied, Lee returned to London again with an additional bounce in his steps, and was then refused the patent for again by the King James I.

King James I

In defeat, Lee and his workers moved their equipment in France however, they did not generate much excitement in France, either. It appeared that Europe was not yet prepared. In any case Lee's frame for stocking is thought to be one of the precursors to what was expected to be the biggest economic and industrial revolution in the course of British time.

In order to understand the events that led to the revolutionary revolution that took place two centuries later it is necessary to revisit the historical events that took place in the period between.

After Lee's death on the 16th of January, in 1614. The threatening pair of political and religious conflicts between Catholic and Protestants escalated and escalated into the Thirty Years' War. The war of the aptly-named Thirty Years' War that lasted for three years, was fought by the armies of the royals from Sweden, Spain, France, Denmark, and the Holy Roman Empire. The much-discussed and unfulfilled accord of Peace of Augsburg, which has just been able to put out the fires of the German religion war, added to the new war. However, what made the difference was the uprising of the Bohemian Protestants. They weren't thrilled with the reign of King Ferdinand II because of their discrimination and the unfair treatment they received from their own people and their animosity was only exacerbated after the Spanish King ordered the desecration of a revered Protestant church in Prague.

King Ferdinand II of Aragon

After the war ended in 1648 John Comenius, Hugo Grotius along with many other German writers who witnessed the horrors of war were determined to leave the tense and narrow-minded historical record the place it belongs - the historical past. They expressed their unwavering dislike of the conflict. Indeed, many were of them believed that the whole ordeal could have been prevented.

This uprising against traditionality couldn't have happened earlier. In the past, almost all of Europe was over each other, hoping to move ahead of the competition in science-based study, exploration and research. This academic revival that had impressed the Europeans with the exciting advances being created by their country's top minds, was accompanied by a variety of terms, like that of Age of Enlightenment, the Age of Reason, and the Scientific Revolution. The desire for science, logic knowledge, understanding, and, more importantly the idea of change was ablaze, and some key players across the globe helping to create that track.

A few of the more well-known name of the time was Galileo Galilei, an intellectual multi-faceted trader who had a key part in the shaping of different scholarly areas during the seventeenth century. Galileo was a zealous student of astronomy, the physics of cosmology, philosophy and mathematicians, and was famously adamant about the theories of Aristotle. One of his best-known discoveries was his reinforced telescope which allowed him to see and examine his rings on Saturn and Jupiter's shining moons as well as other breakthroughs in extraterrestrial science.

Galileo

A lot of these genius minds were based in Britain as well, and in 1620, at the time of a specific increase in popularity and growth of Astronomy the English politician named Francis Bacon Francis Bacon pioneered a method for philosophers and scientists that changed the method by which "truthfulness" or scientific conclusions were evaluated. Bacon was aware that data or deductive reasoning derived by human perception were prone to error and frequently in error. He urged people to question all situations before coming to conclusions using a thorough and controversial technique that employed an "manipulation of nature" and the manipulation of specific factors to reach a certain and undisputed truth.

Bacon

Bacon's innovative scientific methodology could lead to the rise of outside-the-box thinkers who soon became famous. One of them included Sir Isaac Newton, the father of modern physics and gravity and also the first scientist awarded the title of knight in England. The resurgence of modern scientific discoveries also led to the creation of a highly regarded academic society - that of the Royal Society of England. The society, not officially established until the 1660s, consisted of the "invisible college" of natural doctors, philosophers researchers, scientists and others.

In 1663 the society was recognized officially by the crown and was renamed"the "Royal Society of London for Improving Natural Knowledge." "Nullius in verba," is a Latin expression that means "on the word of no one," or "take nobody's word for it," was chosen as the motto for the group. This concise statement was the core of their mission and demonstrated their determination to "withstand the domination of authority" and promote the truths that were uncovered through careful and meticulous research. Today, more than more than 8,000 people have been accepted into the society, ranging from Newton himself, to Charles Darwin, Albert Einstein, Ernest Rutherford, and others who are renowned scientists.

Newton

A major person who came to prominence at this time included Thomas Hobbes, who caused some controversy with the release of his 4 piece epic, Leviathan. The lengthy essay that argued for the commonwealth state that he thought is the sole way to attaining a harmonious society. In order to live in a world that is built upon an inherent basis based on"the "war of every man against man," Hobbes advised that people think about Leviathan as a body that will be led by a ruthless and powerful leader who would beat the materialistic and selfish people to form.

Then, a few years later John Locke aimed to set the record straight in his ideal government, which he wrote in his book Two Treatises of Government, released in 1691. Locke opposed the notion of the divine rights of the kings. Locke believed the monarchs had authority over the rest, given that their royal status was granted by God Almighty. In contrast, Locke endorsed a society built upon "mutual agreement" between the administration and the people. Also that if people did not like the king, they would have every right to hand him the punishment.

The publication of Locke appealed to the masses with the majority of people embracing his views over

Hobbes"conservative" approach to the unity of society. This endorsement only added evidence of the modern and creative mindset that was prevalent who lived in Britain. People were ecstatic about this rapid path to progress, which would be a catalyst for changes.

One of the most important triggers of this Industrial Age was the aftermath of another revolutionary event prior to it but of a different type one that took place in 1688 - it was the Glorious Revolution of 1688. In that revolution when the English Protestants succeeded in stripping the Catholic King James II of his crown and replacing him by the common monarchs of the time, William of Orange as well as King James II's personal child, Mary.

Chapter 2: Portrait Of William And Mary

Following this period was the announcement of the Bill of Rights in 1689 and guaranteed absolute rights and freedoms for everyone Englishmen. The power of the crown was restricted by new rules which included one that prohibited their interference in the elections of Parliament. They also could not implement taxes or legislation without the permission of the government. In addition, the monarchs were not able to establish or supervise their own court. Englishmen had the right to make petitions to for the King, and would never be punished in jail for doing this. Protestants could elect Members of Parliament with no restriction from the king and were able to carry arms. People were spared penalties, forfeitures and imprison without trial by juries, and also from extreme and unjust punishment. The Parliament would be free to make its own decisions and any decisions made by the body were to be finalized and changed inside the institution itself. The law questioned the monarchs who had once been the supreme authority and guaranteed freedom of speech for everyone. It was a clear separation of powers effectively created the first monarchy of constitutional law in Britain.

In 1694, the Queen Mary was stricken with smallpox in 1694. The sorrow of the widowed King only increased the strain of his personal problems. Nation was afflicted by the loss streak of conflicts that he was not content with getting into, but also ordered. These losses were equally humiliating and expensive, to the point that the crown was into bankruptcy, accruing an outstanding amount that was L1.2 million. The saving grace for the monarch in distress was to come from an unlikely source: an unassuming Scottish banker and trader his name William

Paterson, who would offer a solution in the was implemented the same year. Paterson proposed the establishment of the Bank of England, a managed by a private but public institution, that, according to his terms, would "better facilitate the circulation of money...among other inconveniences." The Bank of England, initially with a restricted liability corporation that was responsible for managing the state's finances and was the first private company that was able to legally issue banknotes. After the bank was put established, which was able to in the investigation and repair of the situation with regard to finances in England and the UK, its efficient operation was soon able to compete with the Dutch and, eventually, dominated on the area.

Paterson

Rejuvenated by the technology and stability in the financial market brought to

Britain with the passage of time towards the end of the 18th century the Empire devoted its efforts to fixing its failing manufacturing sector and bolstering its fragile economy. At the time, farming and the raising of sheep was the principal - and, in some areas, the only source of food as well as income. A minimum of 75% of the population were farmers struggling to make the most use as they could farmland. Although the raising of livestock was a common practice and farming equipment was readily at hand, the efficiency of the workplace, aside from British industries overall was still a to be improved.

Prior to drone-shipping, instant global communication, as well as other modern conveniences, the most fundamental of human interactions - which included transporting across towns beyond one's personal 2 feet was an option. In the end, people living in medieval times were typically restricted to their communities and villages. Most food items were manufactured locally, and morale in villages was heavily influenced by the bounty of the harvest seasons. Crop infestations, droughts, and generally poor harvests were not a choice, leaving the farmers and their families with without a choice other than to go cold and long winters. Products were also manufactured locally. Occasionally some products were imported from abroad. The exclusive imports that were transported to London as well as the Bristol ports and Bristol ports, were available only by the upper echelons of the ladder. In spite of the many and diverse technological advancements The majority of the people who lived in the 18th century was not educated. A quality education at prestigious institutions or highly skilled tutors were only available to the rich.

The turn of the century saw it the rise of the cottage business, specifically designed to allow cloth traders to profit from the time off for farmers. If this type of partnership - that typically involved the creation of high-quality textiles starting at the end of the farm - proved productive, it may result in greater profits for merchants of cloth.

This process was as inventive as it was simple. The first step was to distribute raw wool to various farmers on the team. Every family member took part in the process of making cloth. The women scrubbed the wool to remove dirt and then dipped it in dye, and scraped it off with bristles of their nail combs. The fresh wool was transformed into thread using a spinning wheel. The thread was became cloth by weaving it on an loom, undergoing a difficult procedure that demanded more muscle. This was an occupation that usually needed men of the family.

The vendor dropped in during the scheduled hours and picked up the final product before placing them on the marketplace. The potential for profit was huge. earn from this procedure since merchants were able to sell these products made from scrap materials for the price of a good mark-up. The popularity of this industry assisted to boost trade in the nation. This, experts claim helped in preparing our nation for the upcoming revolution.

A flourishing national trade as well as the high demand for British products overseas were just among the numerous catalysts that pushed Britain into the modern age of industrialization. Some also point to its abundance of natural resources and reservoirs. Since Britain historically favored charcoal instead of coal for heat, it was also home to vast deposits of black gold. A lot of which were unexplored. Apart from the coal resources available as well as other precious resources and the "flexible government" brought about through the Glorious Revolution aided in the development of these unconventional ideas.

Many have acknowledged the economic situation of Britain in the early days and its significant part in the revolutionary period. The new bank, along with the rising profits of growing businesses financed some of these ideas and made them ventures. The introduction of promissory note as well as modern credit facilities provided consumers the opportunity to buy more goods and services. The rich that were enjoying the largest slice of pie, became also an avid supporter of the latest concepts and innovations that were thrown from the outside.

Chapter 3: Picking Up Steam

"Should the engine, in be feared by certain people, appear complicated and hard to be worked...I am able to promise them that the present and functioning engine is that far from it, that it is a familiar machine and can be learnt by the people with the least capacities, in small amount of time." ..." -- Thomas Savery, The Miner's Friendship (1702)

The gleeful reactions of the consumers merchants, businessmen, and owners in Britain at the start of the 17th century saw several creators of the competition who gathered to show off their latest products and improved technologies. One of the people who contributed to the march towards technological advancement in the Agricultural Revolution was Jethro Tull from Berkshire and is most famous for tinkering with a marketable engine-driven seed drill around the beginning of the century.

Tull

The seeds were sprayed into the furrows, or into long and narrow trenches that were dug with a hand. It is to be expected that the seeds were typically treated with a lack of finesse at the close of the day that was only naturally as fatigue of farmers increased with each passing hour. This in turn reduced the development of seeds.

Tull was instructing his employees to pay more attention when maintaining the seeds in the guidelines, but as the requests of Tull were not met and he was forced to make the decision on his own control. In 1701 Tull developed a unique drill that was fitted with a moving cylindrical device that could quickly plant seeds into neat rows in one step. Seeds that went through the hopper passed through grooves cut into the cylinder landing on the funnel. The funnel then inserted seeds inside the fresh furrows dug by the plowing appendage that is attached to the back part of the drill. The drill would be manually operated by means of sturdy handles which were employed to control the drill. In addition to making this approach more effective and economical It also created smaller garbage.

Seed drill

Tull is also believed to be responsible for designing the hoe drawn by horses. The description of the hoe is in his book Horse-Hoeing Husbandry. The hoe, offered for sale at L7.50 (roughly $1,457 currently) per piece is essentially an machine with 6 legs. 5 spades, plows, and other equipment, and a wheel. The hoe came with identical handles, however it was able to be altered to suit the needs of a horse. The device was advertised as the fastest method to remove the weeds, unwanted shrubs as well as limp grass and others unwanted growths that were a nuisance on the soil. It took a lot of responsibility off the shoulders of the farmer which meant that he could now be accountable for the operation of the machine as well as sweeping the path of dead branches and leaves that the hoe left on its way.

England was once again in the history books in 1702 by launching The Daily Courant, the first daily national newspaper in the country. It was published by a bookseller and printer Elizabeth Mallet (in other sources, Edward Mallet). Mallet had a beautiful office on Fleet Street, published the project with a more feminine title that was more appealing to the stale attitude of the time: E. Mallet.

The paper pledged to publish only verified information "daily and impartially." The writers of the article also committed to not "[taking] it upon [themselves] to give any comments or conjectures of [their] own, but will relate only matter of fact; supposing other people to have sense enough to make reflections for themselves." For the first time in history that the citizens of Britain had access to major events and notifications on a regular schedule, transforming the character of British communications forever.

In the meantime, the most brilliant minds of Europe began to think about an additional hot subject - invention of a practical power source. In the summer of 1698 the innovator Thomas Savery submitted a patent for an "semi-omnipotent" and "water-commanding" device, referred to the "steam engine." Savery was a name that was buried by the haze of stories and gossip. Due to the apparent similarities in the design of Savery as well as Edward Somerset, the Marquis of Worcester Many accused Savery for stealing the concept and then declaring it his own. Many went as in saying that Savery was trying to erase all evidence of the "borrowed" ideas, tore through the town, bought each of Somerset's novels then burned the books. No matter what, Savery went on to start a ferocious campaign to market his gadget as a pumping machine and even wrote an ebook to highlight its most appealing selling points: The Miner's Friend or A description of an engine to Bring the level of water By fire. Savery was hoping to get more of his revenue from miners as the only person he knew of the capacity to make up the need in the mining industry.

Savery

Growing demands for coal led to deeper mines were required been excavated. However, miners faced an entirely new challenge - flooding. To solve the issue mining workers used horses-powered pumps, which hurriedly dragged an entire bucket of water at each time from the earth. Although they were useful in a limited degree, it was an exhausting process it was only efficient for mines not more than 90 feet deep. Savery offered his engine as a solution for this problem, and could be utilized to efficiently pump water from the mines. Although it sounded tempting but the miners were unable to warm their feet and feared the possibility of explosions coming from the boilers or receivers that were nearby. Although Savery's engine was never turned off during the mining sector, the device served to deliver the water needed to cities and some other private institutions.

Pump of Savery

In 1712, self-described ironmonger Thomas Newcomen, squeezed his way into the limelight by introducing his own take on the Savery's "crude" steam pumping engine. Newcomen's modified engine would be recognized as the world's most first "practical steam engine" for the fact that it had a piston. The engine's improved design was created with the removal of coal-mine water with the intention of removing coal mine water.

The Newcomen engine created an air vacuum within a piston using condensed steam generated by the boiler. The force produced by steam was the catalyst that activated and forced the piston to move inside of it. The rhythmic motion of the piston. The piston was connected to a rocker arms that was linked to a pump that gradually drew the water out of the ground.

Doing not want to get into the shoes of Savery, who had been known to be quick to defend any patent-related matter, Newcomen hesitantly brought Savery into the conversation. The initial engine Newcomen offered was placed in a mine that was coal-based, it came with a cylindrical that was 8 feet long and 21 inches wide. It was powered by 12 pumps per minute and was able to draw about 10 gallons of water from an underground mine running 156-ft deep. Although no one was able to find an issue with the reliability of the engine but it did been more expensive than it's worth, however, there were at most 100 machines operating at Newcomen's demise in 1729.

Different fields within the business also started to discover the benefits of coal. It was not just abundant, but it was also discovered coal needed less work to mine contrast to the alternative which was a more lengthy process which involved the creation of charcoal of shredded wood. From a financial standpoint, local coal mining was the most viable choice that time. The other European nations had no alternative than to ship coal in trains and the cost of transport surpassing the value at when the goods arrived at its location. In contrast most coal mines located in Britain were located on the coast. Domestic coal shipments to London which was the capital of England was significantly lower.

Metal industry was one of the first industries to recognize the power of coal. It was not long before they as well, began to incorporate coal into the process of melting. Smelting (extracting minerals from stones by heat and melt) of coal an idea which existed from 1678. However, it was only going to flourish in the Industrial Age.

Following years and years of unsuccessful experiments and failures, in 1680 Sir Clement Clerke finally succeeded in melting lead using a coal-fueled "reverberatory furnace," otherwise called"cupola "cupola," in Bristol. Eight years later the same success was repeated at Upper Redbrook, this time by using copper. Utilizing coal for smelting was quickly adopted by blacksmiths as well as metallurgical enthusiasts from all over the country because it was observed that the impurities of the heating material, such as sulfur ash, never infiltrated the smelted iron making for the product to be cleaner and better quality.

In the end, this was not the end of the story.

Chapter 4: New Paths And Fresh Avenues

"For the beginning of something brand new is to occur, it has to take place a. Newton witnessed an apple fall; James Watt watched a boiling kettle; Roentgen fouled some photographic plates. They were able to transform everyday events into something fresh ..." Sir Alexander Fleming

In order to ensure the country's economic stability In order to ensure the stability of its economy, Parliament passed a number of preemptive measures that targeted arrival of imports coming from competitors who were close to them. One example is those Calico Acts of 1700 and 1721 which impeded imports of foreign products predominantly originated from India and protected the silk, wool as well as other areas of the British textile sector. They were aware of the negative results of the "calico craze" from India in the past century and in the background when it devastated the neighboring European countries as well as within the country itself. The time was right to put a stop to it down.

The 1600s saw the silk and cotton textiles with exotic and vibrant patterns that were referred to as "calico," were flying from the stores in East Indian Companies. This rapid increase in demand for the fabric had already taken a noticeable effect on European industries of textiles. The demand for calico was sweeping across British border and led to the escalating number of closures of local shops for textiles which prompted Parliament to ban nearly all imported products.

Other related laws were passed over the years. While the prohibition ended in 1774 textiles, calicos as well as other products that came from India were subject to heavy duty that raised eyebrows up through the mid-1820s. There was a common belief that the laws enacted by the Parliament gave British entrepreneurs and merchants the ability to investigate and play with innovative designs in the industry of textiles.

It was in 1719 that Thomas Lombe, a resident in Derby, England, founded an industrial silk-throwing plant, called Lombe's Mill that was which was the initial "continuous production unit" in the world. Silk-throwing was an invention of weaving in Italy in the 13th century. It involved weaving silk threads in order to make a stronger yarn that was multi-threaded. In order to keep their advantage in the marketplace, the Italian designers wisely decided to remain secret about their precious method. In bringing this technology into Britain, Lombe knew, was a challenge.

Lombe's Mill

The legend says that Lombe wanted to find an companion in his brother John who was born four years before. John was the ideal partner since he worked at an Italian establishments that contained the machine which was specifically designed for this job. Over the next couple of months, when midnight rolled around John went back to his work area with a the pen, paper and lamps in his hands. In the quiet and empty work area the worker sat near the machine for silk throwing and carefully sketched an elaborate drawing of the device using the flickering light from his lamp.

The diagrams had been smuggled back to Britain before 1716. two years later Thomas registered a patent on the patent, which was referred to by the name of "A New Invention of Three Sorts of Engines Never Before Made or Used in Great

Britain." The first covered the spinning of "finest raw silk." The other was focused on weaving raw silk as well as the silk braiding, that was referred to by the name of "organzine."

Lancashire quickly gained the attention of others in the British cotton industry. It was a county that was already gaining respectable status in wool production, had all the essential elements which allowed it to rule the market. Lancashire was a place of moist weather and fertile soils and was the perfect environment for processing and storage of the finicky cotton threads. They generally lost moisture and became dry in places that absorbed only dry heat. The proximity of water to the town also provided plenty of juice for the mills that were powered by water in the town.

Some have attributed the Lancashire's success in the field of textiles because of the revolutionary technology that was introduced to the industry during that time. It was in 1733 that John Kay, an engineer, inventor, and engineer, received patents for"the "New Engine for Opening and Dressing Wool," an machine known for its basic and revolutionary component: the shuttle that flew. This flying machine was a small but vital component that gave an efficient way to tax the process of moving the manual shuttle in a circular motion in order to transfer the weft, or crosswise threads on the warp (threads which overlapped, and then put under weft threads for the production of cloth). Kay's shuttle, which was a wood double-pointed and palm-sized device with mini rollers, was able to perform this task completely, meaning that weavers did not have to operate the shuttle by hand in any way.

Audrias Meskauskas' photo of a shuttle that's flying

Manufacturers of clothing, particularly the ones who were focused on wool, were thrilled with this invention as it drastically accelerated the process of weaving. However, the popularity of wool was not without consequences. Weavers that were employed to operate these shuttles had their time reduced, or they were removed from the process.

If he was planning to or whether he had intended to or Kay ended up being the center of newly laid-off workers who reacted with anger. In addition the manufacturers were unable to provide Kay the royalty he believed that he was entitled to. Dissatisfied with the way they treated him, Kay loaded his sensational shuttles in his car and headed for France. And, even more disappointingly the shuttle was greeted with what is best called a sluggish applause to say the least. The process took two times as much persuasion of Kay's side to get the French finally agreed to try the product. Kay was killed in the midst of an endless and tiring fight for royalties. dues to him from producers across Britain not being paid.

Following was a succession of innovators trying to duplicate the previous huge success. In the late 18th century, large-scale production in the textile industry was at its highest and with it the huge demand for more thread. It was in 1764 that James Hargreaves made it his goal to come up with solutions to satisfy the increasing demand. Hargreaves' name was the basis of Hargreaves' invention was believed to have been result of an eureka moment. The daughter of his, Jenny, had unintentionally fallen over his wheel. Its spindle was able to pop out and soaring throughout the room. Hargreaves was captivated to the captivating view of the spinning wheel when it was rolling over the flooring. That was the moment when he realized the spindle might be a clue to something. The spinning jenny came into existence. In the present, the tale has been cast aside as a falsehood, and other sources claim that Jenny was actually the name given to his wife.

The spinning jenny

The spinning jenny is a hand-powered machine for spinning that had 8 spindles. It simulated the pace and output of eight weavers at the same time. Much like the fying shuttle although the spinning jenny was an instant hit with producers across the city however, it was the cause of the ire of weavers, who's livelihoods are at risk of slipping away from a fragile chain that was threatening to break in the blink of an eye. Hargreaves had to move to Nottingham in order to avoid the controversy. Six years later, Hargreaves was granted another patent to design a new spinning jenny that had more spindles. Hargreaves' time was spent in pursuing legal actions against the people whom he believed had copied his ideas.

In the early 1760s, Richard Arkwright, a barber and hair-maker from Bolton met John Kay and Thomas Highs. The conversation grew more lively, Kay and Highs confided to Arkwright about a spin machine that they were in development. Incredulous, Arkwright's ears perked as he took a deep breath and sat on their each phrase. While he was listening and learned more about the reasons of the project's demise simply put, they had broken. Three of them parted ways as the conversation slowed down however, Arkwright felt the tingle in his sleeves. Arkwright went to Kay by himself and offered to revive the plan, with Highs removed from the image. The desperate Kay was willing to accept, because Kay knew that it was only going to be the case of time, earlier than he anticipated and even before somebody took him down. Others from the local craft community were employed and a schoolhouse was rented for the purpose of finishing what had been begun.

The project team was subject to a confidentiality agreement which is why they kept their words a secret for the duration of the work. This did not keep the sound of their machinery and tools to leak out from the thin wafer walls. The neighbors who believed that they were not doing evil began spreading the word about their activities. Some gossipers believed that witchcraft and black magic was happening behind shut doorways.

Arkwright

It was in 1768 that Arkwright together with his group revealed a frame for spinning that contained three sets of rollers which were able to rotate at different speed. The Arkwright rollers could not only make yarn that was consistent in thickness, but they also bettered the yarn spun by spinning jennys in terms of strength and flexibility. Arkwright then went on to establish Britain's first cotton mill, located in Cromford.

Arkwright's spinning frames, which were patent-pending, were connected to and powered through a water wheel which is why they are called"water frame. "water frame," which produced more force than manual driven wheels. In this regard even though the yarn spun from the water frame were stronger than that of those made by the Hargreaves brand and was most suitable for warp threads but it was not able to increase speed or reduce the amount of the amount of manpower required, since they could only hold just one thread at the time.

The year 1779 was when Samuel Crompton decided to combine the best of the two worlds. He combined elements of the spinning jenny as well as the frame for water, creating the hybrid weave marvel called"the "spinning mule." On on top of having 1,320 spindles of spinning, the mules utilized Jenny's rotating rolling carriage as well as rollers that were that were similar to the ones used for the water frame which enabled the spinning of various yarns with a variety of textures and thicknesses.

Not surprising, to say the spinning mule didn't get the approval of the general public would be a huge understatement. People who were working from home worried about the demise of their cottage business. All kinds of families depended on these enterprises, for the majority of them this was the only source of butter and bread. Over time, tensions increased, leading to violent riots that broke out to demonstrate violent protests. This included the Luddite Rebellion of 1811-1816.

In the late 18th century, the more inventive inventors that had an affinity with manufacturing made further advancements to technology that was outdated throughout all of the important industries. The area around the Severn River had become a center of iron production. It was then that Darby and the Darby family. A clan that was a pioneering group soon to be the iron mavens of their time. in 1709 Abraham Darby chose to continue the place Clemente Clerke had left off. He realized that coke, mostly carbon residues from "incomplete combustion" or heating of coal, could be utilized in lieu of charcoal to smelt Pig iron, which is one of the constituents of cast iron products and other products. Darby immediately patented his coke-based Pig iron and quickly began to surpass other retailers by selling pig iron cookware kettles, kettles and various kitchen products. The public was attracted by Darby's goods because they were more durable, thinner and most important of all affordable.

Darby II, his son Darby II, inherited his father's method for coke fueling, which was used to make cast iron. In the early days, the coke-based pig iron was less expensive than charcoal equivalent, and since casting iron was now cheap enough being used for building materials. It was in 1777 that Darby III took advantage of the growing popularity of cast iron, and employed it to construct the magnificent Iron Bridge, a powerful arch-shaped beauty which hung above the Severn.

In the latter half of the 1700s, Henry Cort also began to try out wrought iron to cast conversion strategies to the testing. Traditionally, blacksmiths were required perform the conversion by hitting the iron using a trap hammer. The year 1783 was when Cort developed a new device that had "grooved rollers" that removed all hammering out of the problem. The new method was believed to have been fifteen times more efficient than the old trap-hammering method. Also, it was better suited to forming thin and smooth sheet of steel. It was later improved to accommodate angular shapes and other curly shapes.

In the following one was in the year Cort invented the puddling method, which involved mixing of pig iron that was molten inside a reverberatory oven. Puddling iron is denser and was more malleable, and durable than iron pig, and was perfectly created for his rollers. But the creation of puddled iron wasn't an simple job. It was a painful and exhausting job and it was believed that puddlers were not able for 40 years.

It's no surprise that Newcomen's steam engine was also in need to be updated, which was the catalyst that brought one of the Revolution's most famous names onto the central scene. The model from the models of Newcomen was given to James Watt, a low-ranking scientist in the department of Physics at Glasgow's University of Glasgow. Watt was given the task of helping fix the engine that was malfunctioning, while tinkering on his model, he became shocked by the amount of steam was required for it to work. Watt knew that there must find a more efficient method.

Watt

Watt was searching for a solution for months. It took until May next year when it was finally revealed upon his. Newcomen's design was built around the same cylinder which played two different functions: it received steam inflow at its highest pressure, it then condensed into an air vacuum, which would then spur the cylinder to motion. Watt decided to build a second connecting chamber that he named"a "condenser," outside of the chamber. A water spout was then pumped out through the new space, forming the condenser's vacuum.

Five years later, Watt applied for a patent on the condenser which would later be a crucial component of the future steam engines. The 1780s were the time when Watt introduced two further improvements in the design of steam engines. One was a double-acting machine, with a piston that was able to pull and push with less effort, which was extremely useful in operating machines. The year 1788 was when Watt created the governor centrifugal. It was utilized to control the engine's speed by adjusting the amount of fuel was pumped into the engine's cylinders.

Watt, who was working an unpaid job at the school at the start of his path, required help in obtaining funding. In this regard, he turned towards Matthew Boulton, the son of a stamper who worked in silver from Birmingham who was now an entrepreneur who was successful on his own. Alongside his financial backing and being Watt's sales and production channel over the following 11 years Boulton was also a role in the development of new steam engines. Around 1800 the number of engines was more than 500 steam engines in operation all over the world.

Revolutionary times also gave an opportunity to revamp the transportation system of the country and cities' infrastructure. In the early 17th century the vast majority of British roads were just plain paintings of hard, uneven dirt. The roads of the early days were susceptible to drastic changes that were dictated by weather. When winter was frosty it was more than twice as hard to keep them on their feet in the slick wet sludge underneath their feet. On hot summer days the people were forced to choose of battling the bumpy and muddy surface. Parishes were the ones responsible in the care and maintenance of these roads, and they had required to be maintained six every year. Because the streets - specifically major roads which connected cities were not used as often the maintenance rate was low that did not help improve the condition of the roads.

The roads that were shaky and unstable were meant for walking. But transporting fragile items proved to be a problem at a different level. Glass, ceramics as well as other broken items inside the mule-driven dragons would often be nearly completely destroyed before they traveled to their final destinations. It wasn't just a pathetic waste of material and energy, but it increased prices for the remaining things. As the country was reintroduced to mass production in the Industrial Revolution, the unstable and unorganized roads were overloaded with mules carrying products that the Parliament was forced to intervene.

In 1663, the Parliament approved in 1663 the initial Turnpike Act and tested out the new system across three counties. The authorities were instructed to construct toll gates where they could charge fees to people who traveled on major roads within their county. These funds would then be used exclusively for the urgently needed reconstruction of roadways that were once in use. After the system was judged feasible, the Parliament erected the gates tolls across Britain.

As the roads improved across the entire country but not everybody was happy with the increased costs. There were those who yelled highway robbery. protested against the system by running past drivers and jumping across the gates to pay. Therefore, spikes or, as they were called in the past, "pikes," were put on the tops of the gates.

Thomas Telford is one of those who are often blamed for an improvement in British construction. It is said that he would be the architect of around 920 miles roads during his lifetime. In the role of Telford was known as the "Colossus of Roads," Telford was praised for his calculations and observations about angles, slopes layout, traffic and all the way to the width of road material. One of his most memorable tasks included the re-construction of the London Bridge in the 19th century. He also worked on the creation of the Caledonian Canal, which connected Inverness with Corpach within Scotland.

Chapter 5: Telford

James Brindley was yet another winner of the construction industry. In 1759, Brindley was invited by the Duke of Bridgewater to a private gathering. The duke wanted to find a more economical method of transporting the coal from his mine into Manchester. According to the Duke that it could be achieved through the construction of a canal or artificial river that permitted vessels to pass through - connected with the Irwell River, roughly 3 miles away from the mine.

The duke was delighted, Brindley declared that he could make him better. He proposed a longer canal which would join the Aqueduct (waterway bridge) over the Irwell River and run straight towards Manchester just 10 miles from the city. The mid-July 1761 date was when the canal, which later came to be known by the name of Bridgewater Canal, was officially accessible to the public. It was the only British canal to allow water transport without the aid of natural rivers. The Bridgewater Canal was an early example of Canal Acts to be approved. A variety of similar projects and laws quickly followed, including the Trent and Mersey Canal, constructed five years later; for the Forth and Clyde in 1768 as well as the Leeds and Liverpool Canal, completed in 1770.

Nuts and Bolts

"Science is the great antidote to the poison of enthusiasm and superstition." -- Adam Smith, The Wealth of Nations

The wave of academic as well as political and industrial revolutions spread across Europe, the intellectuals from all over the world separated themselves from the masses and started to establish clubs that were their own. One of them was called the Lunar Circle, otherwise known as the "Lunar Society," based in Birmingham. The club was exclusive, and was home to just 14 members included some of the most revered scientists, engineers and inventors in England.

The meetings, which ran from 1765 until 1813 took place in the house of one of the co-founders, Matthew Boulton. Like the name suggests it was a place to meet on the Mondays that were closest to full moon. The underground gatherings were usually set for the late evening hours with the light of the full moon illuminated the trails that lead the participants home. The club also had other members who comprised Watt, Erasmus Darwin, an acclaimed botanist, inventor, and the grandpa of Charles Darwin, and Josiah Wedgwood the pioneer of pottery as well as Darwin's second grandfather and many other people. The combined efforts of these men could propel this Industrial Revolution to heights that did not even the most awestruck observers see coming.

In the latter half of the 1700s, yet another industry field came into the spotlight that of tool and machine manufacturing. The first names to emerge from this industry was John Wilkinson. He was born in 1761. Wilkinson along with his twin brother acquired their father's iron mill located in Bersham. It was the New Bersham Company, as it was named at the time as, was made the leading maker of top-quality guns, and was hailed for their guns castings and cannons.

Wilkinson

The year 1774 was the time Wilkinson one who discovered the bug of invention himself and filed for a patent on the "boring engine," which could revolutionize cannonry. Before the boring stage the old cannons were initially made (the process of pouring molten substances into molds) then topped by a core that contained an internal mold that was used to fill in any gaps that were left behind by the cast. The engine of Wilkinson, which turned the barrel of the gun instead it was able to increase the accuracy of the cannon's balls, and reduced the detonation rate.

This engine was later employed to bore the pistons of Watt and Boulton's steam engines. Wilkinson's firm also made parts for the cylinders as well as other equipment used by the duo for over more than 20 years. Then, Wilkinson was issued another patent for the spiral grooves he made into cannons. This increased the accuracy and distance of the cannon ball. Wilkinson died wealthy, and was buried in a beautiful iron coffin.

The height of British inventions in toolmaking would be at the beginning of the 19th century. Henry Maudslay, from Woolwich, Kent, was practically born to drilling machines and roaring noises. He began his work when he was 12 as a powder monkey collecting gunpowder in cartridges over and over again. A couple of months later, he enrolled to become a blacksmith, and then worked to perfect his construction techniques. By the age of 18 he was recruited to develop the initial "unpickable" lock.

The thing that would really make his name appear on the map was the invention of the lathe that cut screws. The huge machine made of metal made uniform screws in massive quantities and improved the efficacy and triumphs that followed the Industrial Revolution. The lathes might have existed before Maudslay's time however his designs with gearshifts as well as a slide-rest and lead screws, was unbeatable for their the durability and usefulness.

The 18th century was drawing to an end and the 18th century came to an end, it became clear that it was clear that the Industrial Revolution in Britain was currently at its peak. At the close of the 17th century, Great Britain had churned out more than L2.5 billion in today's local-made goods. The production of coal was now an enormous industry and it was growing at a rapid rate. In order to put it in perspective, 2.7 million tons of coal were extracted in the year the year 1700. One century later, the number was soaring to 10 million but it was not yet at the apex of its growth. A century later, the figure was 250 million.

In 1801 on Christmas Eve The inhabitants from Camborne, England wandered out of their houses and stores with their eyes giddy with amazement. The front part of an train sitting on a wagon that had four wheels and steam gushing through its heavy cylinder, was seen just around the corner. While the mysterious locomotive made along the road with its seven beaming passengers, they saluted the people. The enigmatic design was nothing less that the Richard Trevithick's "Puffing Devil," the first "steam-powered passenger vehicle." The Devil was able to climb hills according to one of its riders described, "like a little bird...going faster than I could walk." The Devil caught fire after it overheated a few days after the first appearance, however, aside from the incident the impression was that it was about to get off in a good direction.

Chris Allen's photo depicts a re-creation of the devil who puffs

The Middling Sort and the Invisible Cogs

"I sell here, sir, what all the world desires to have - power." Matthew Boulton, 1776. Matthew Boulton, 1776

After the discovery of steam power as well as similar innovations, British cities were fast expanding. Once barren, the areas were now filled with more however, but bigger plots of factory as well as its tall and impressive structures rising in awe all over the cityscape. In addition, the population grew in the same way. Many hopefuls came into the city from the surrounding countryside, making a plethora of applications to be employed in factories. Together, the cities in Salsford and

Manchester were home to 25,000 people at the time of 1772. Within just a few years, that population had grown to 181,000 and, thirty years later, it was at 455,000.

Birmingham was among the cities with the greatest power across Britain in the time of. In contrast to Lancashire which was the capital city of the trade in textiles, Birmingham was a robust yet groovy city in the forefront of energy development and development, due to its abundant reservoirs of wood, coal and iron. Birmingham was the city that would catch interest of the general public in the middle of the 19th century when the Birmingham railway, that linked Birmingham to London and was built.

While Birmingham might have been a hive in activities, Alexis de Tocqueville painted more of a dark picture of the distant and mechanical city. According to the French visitors, it was merely the sound of an "immense workshop, a huge forge" that was able to find "busy people and faces brown with smoke," which was set against the unending hum that consisted of "nothing but the sound of hammers, and the whistle of steam escaping boilers."

The growing British economy was the catalyst for what is now known as the Victorian middle class, or according to the terminology of that time, the "middling sort." This was a reference to the group of people that were wedged between the aristocracy of England and the lower classes of Britain. The 19th century was when the middle class of Britain was at its most affluent and the most diverse yet.

Alongside the top manufacturers were entrepreneurs with small fry who put the smallest stalls and shops that were their own. They succeeded in developing niche markets in order to avoid clashing against those who competed in the major leagues. Profits boosted all British firms helped to fund railways, ships and insurance and banks that were part of the empire's industrial.

The newly formed middle class enjoyed the advantages of their recent economic prosperity. After the passing of laws that cut down on working hours the people had an extra hour of relaxation. Pubs began popping in the United States and established itself as the popular place to socialize for working and middle classes that were unable to resist their cheap menus. The time was made available to let people complete their studies or study in specialized areas of study and pursuits. Some dressed to enjoy a night out at the club, dining in fancy restaurants, and visiting the theaters.

Merchants and manufacturers all over Britain took advantage of the chance to profit from the mediocre type's latest spending money. Print and handwritten posters, leaflets as well as other types of Victorian advertisement were released for the general public. In the latter part of the 19th century, advertisements began to be more inventive. Many dressed their shop windows with attractive signs to highlight their latest items and also other top-selling products. Other businesses rented slots to customers in newspapers and billboards. One advertisement showed a fashionable and attractive couple sitting standing on a balcony, drinking warm cup from Cadbury's Cocoa Drink in hand as they looked out at the stunning scene of the river beneath the river. Another poster for Pears' Soap showed a gorgeous, plump lady with supple and fair skin. She was washing her hands elegantly in the basin.

The growth of middle class as well as the abundance of money to spend contributed to the rapid growth of factories. One of the earliest, perhaps the first large-scale manufacturing facilities that was in existence is that of the Soho Foundry, founded by Watt, Boulton, and their brothers. The company was founded in Smethwick near Birmingham in 1796, it produced steam engines they created and perfected. In the following years, the business was expanded to include gas-lighting machines steamships, marine engines.

William Brunton was appointed foreman in the workshop chain. Brunton later proceeded to create a device to cut, mold and form the teeth on the wheels of machinery. It also used steam-powered mint equipment and became so popular that it was later shipped into ports all the way to Russia, Mexico, and India. In its peak, the Soho Foundry was one of the biggest factories worldwide, housing hundreds of employees into numerous rooms within the three-story building. It is believed that the factory have been an amazing thing that it was the destination of choice for many European high-ranking officials, who frequently stopped at Birmingham to have a glimpse of the Soho Foundry firsthand.

In the next few months, the factory was at the forefront of attracting tours of its own. Tourists from all over all over the world came to Birmingham for a visit to the Soho Foundry and the city's impressive array of manufacturing facilities. The visitors were amazed at the stunning modern machinery, which churns out goods at significantly faster and at a lower cost than before.

The same way, Victorian card advertisements were distributed in a similar manner, attached to the walls, then on the streets in the form of breadcrumbs for tourists who wandered around. The first one advertised the best range of knives made by William Harvey, products certified and accepted from "His Majesty's Honorable Board of Ordnance." Another one by B.H. Harris advertised "telescopal toasting forks," which were forks with a double pronged extension designed for toasting marshmallows, wieners, and other sweets.

People were amazed at the ability of manufacturers to make the tiniest, stunning of baubles and ornaments. Local silversmith and goldsmith, J. Taylor, made use of steam-powered equipment to create exquisite buttons made of ivory, tortoiseshell and the iridescent material that adorned the mollusk's inner shell that is known by the name of "mother-of-pearls." Even more appealing were the "Birmingham's Toys," which attracted crowds after crowds of people. These unique toys were not you slept in at night, but small metal trinkets that were kept in the crook of the grip. They could be that were slung around necks or placed in pockets, and kept in their pockets throughout the day. An example of this was the snuff box that was an evocative of tiny mint tins that carried snuff, also known as powdered tobacco smokes, in the compartment. Another toy of renown was the vinaigrette. They were ornamental containers that held smelling salts as well as other scents. These were extremely useful in the event of traveling in filthy, polluted environments and also for sneaking in an aroma in the presence of a sour-smelling friend.

The industrial boom resulted in significant changes to the working population. A declining cottage industry forced couples and single women to seek work away from their houses, with the bulk of them looking for work in factories. Women were most likely to find work as domestic workers and in production of textiles. A part of them were employed in mines for coal.

The modern machinery and advancements that were developed during the period of revolution also created significant changes to the industry in terms of gender separation. In the past, women tended to be spinning, since they were believed to be "trained with more dexterity" than males, whereas muscles of men were put to use in different areas. In the Industrial Revolution, women were responsible for operating light equipment including water frames as well as spinning jennys. The males were responsible for spinning mules. If women from Glasgow finally began spin mules on their own and began to spin mules, they received brutal attacks by male workers that felt their job was under threat.

Certain British women were happy with the coming of age of independence and independent earnings stable, security, and better living standards which came along with the change. Writers Ivy Pinchbeck and Frederick Engels declared that women of working class considered themselves "emancipated" by the inclusion this was long-overdue.

The time also provided the opportunity to an army of female inventors. One of the women inventors included Eleanor Coade of Exeter, creator of the Coade Artificial Stone Company and one of the first female entrepreneurs in the whole of Britain. Eleanor was a skilled artist, created a brand new kind of ceramic that was named the "Coade stone." This comprised crushed glass, clay silicates and terracotta that were cooked in kilns that were hot and blistering.

Another one was Anna Maria Garthwaite of Lincolnshire A prolific queen of textiles who specialized in silk and floral patterns. Garthwaite alone was able to design hundreds of unique pattern designs in textiles. She produced every year around 80 designs during the peak of her profession in the 1740s.

However, the positive feelings were not shared by the majority of women. The first thing to note is that the majority of factories were disgustingly filthy and dirty, as well as the working environment was awful. Women complained that their family life and education affected by their gruelling and non-negotiable timetables. The males were generally given more responsibilities than women despite their absence of experience or expertise and they were paid more earnings for the same volume of work.

Alice Clark, a British historian from the UK, claimed that Industrial Revolution actually impeded the development of women. As per Clark, British women in the 16th century were active in trade as well as agriculture. The majority of women were masters of their home and also their factories in the industry of cottages. Women whose husbands were occupied with travelling business held the forts, directing farm businesses at home, the family business and estates. Women had a better chance of equality than they had ever been before, but although not much, it was a significant step towards equality.

But, as it was time for the Industrial Revolution dawned, women were thrown back onto the slope of development. Men quit their homes for work in factories which left women in charge of unpaid tasks. The middle class women found themselves in a disconcerting situation, as they were not required to do any work but given the dreary chore of directing the housekeepers. The women of the lower class that resigned themselves to the job became depressed because there were no options for them to take to stop being underpaid or overworked.

The tremendous growth rate that factories and manufacturing facilities in Britain saw was like the cursed coin which concealed a negative aspect. Apart from women, thousands of kids worked in the plants, factories and mills. Some manufacturers would even prefer children because they were an affordable hiring option. Also, children were easier to marshal because, at one time, 40 percent of the population of England were younger than 16. Orphans were also a popular choice for employers because they could be easily swept away, and replaced easily if need to.

While these factories were as productive as they were, their working conditions were unimaginable. The regular shifts were 12- 14 hours with the exception of time off. Also, there were differences in wages. The average male worker made about 75 cents ($62.40 USD) while women earned paid just 35 pence ($29.12) while children earned about $12.48. In addition to this barely living wage and fines for the tiniest of insignificant of offences, like the act of whistling, daydreaming or putting an extra bit of dirt at one's work place, were handed to the workers. A few workers claimed that their employers were manipulating clocks to ensure they could get punished for lateness.

The workers were also subject to cruel punishment, with the most frequent being the strapping of fastened with leather straps. Children faced the same kind of torture and those who acted in a manner that was unruly or did not perform standard were required to wear weights made of iron on their necks. Some were lowered into baskets, then hung off the ceiling in order to inspire people into working hard. A few had their ears, but not their fingers as they affect their work attached to tables in the workshop.

The children were also subjected to numerous dangers as a result of their jobs and often involved cleaning under or within the machinery that was not secured properly. Many hundreds, if not thousands of kids were hurt or killed while working. In addition, stepping outside into cold, dark air following an all day inside the stale factory, hot and humid environment caused an increase in the number of pneumonia cases, as well as the spewed dust from factories resulted in lung cancer and other respiratory ailments.

The living conditions beyond the walls of the factory were not more hospitable. A swarm of people crammed in shabby and poorly lit houses with a lot of houses lacking the luxury of running water or light. The air was contaminated and the gutters were filled with garbage and animal manure as well as wastewater, which created breeding grounds for typhus, cholera tuberculosis, as well as a multitude of others.

It didn't take the long time it took to get British workers to voice their concerns against the sexism and the Parliament took the fight, although with a slew of changes that could be horrifying to the people. The year 1799 was the year that Prime Secretary William Pitt the Younger published the first of the Combination Acts, which prohibited the unionization of workers to form unions. "Badgering" employers for shorter work hours, battling for a higher pay and any additional rights that were rightfully earned were no longer a possibility.

Chapter 6: William Pitt The Younger

Another aspect of the darker side of the Industrial Revolution was the British slave trade. British slave owners and traders were among the wealthy in the Industrial Age. It was no surprise when over 2.5 million slaves shackled and imprisoned like animals transported over the violent and insecure waters in the Atlantic. Once the slaves got to the shore, they were forced into factory and plantations to endure long periods of hard and unpaid labour. Any profits, however unsavory that were earned from slave trading are believed to have gone to fund banks, libraries, as well as other places of public use. They also claimed to have been used to finance Watt's research into steam engines and other areas to help develop British industry. Many went so far as to suggest that slavery trade was the primary factor to an Industrial Revolution.

Fortunately, the slavery trade quickly caught the eye of human rights advocates. British Abolitionists quickly began to campaign to end the abominable way of life. As time passed, their efforts eventually were rewarded. The 25th March of 1807 was the day that it was the day that the Abolition of the Act on Slaves Trade was declared the savage human exchange as unlawful throughout the British colonies.

Road to Reform

"Man is the creature of circumstances." -- Robert Owen, The Life of Robert Owen, 1857

In tandem with steam engines, which were an emblem that embodies the Industrial Revolution, the new time of economic and commercial prosperity also brought about an British railway sector. It was in 1767 that Richard Reynolds of Coalbrookdale invented the first track for railways using the wooden rails he built, which then were transformed into iron. The benchmark for railroad innovation was set the moment that the coal's first load was moved through Reynolds track. In the beginning of the 19th century parliament passed an act allowing the construction of the first "railway." The wooden tracks were laid out slowly across London and carried carts powered by horses and mules.

In 1813, twelve years after the revealing of the Trevithick's Puffing Devil, William Hedley unveiled his version of the steam-run engine with the Puffing Billy, which was specifically designed for use in mines. It was a mine-specific locomotive. Puffing Billy replaced horses with an electric coal wagon which operated on shiny steel tracks. Although the Billy was able to travel at a speed of 5 mph, it established the basis for future developments in coal transport.

Hedley

The next the year George Stephenson, known by his admirers as the "father of the British railways," submitted an application to patent the Blutcher chain of eight cars that could transport as much as 30 tonnes of coal. The Blutcher was the first steam-powered locomotive to operate through public rail lines. The Blutcher was launched at the speed of four miles an hour, however Stephenson was quick to get it working to increase the speed. The train, built by Stephenson in 1825 named the "Locomotion," was taken to a test run. It was a successful test like Stephenson wanted, was completed without a hitch, carrying more than 450 passengers between Darlington until

Stockton station with a rate of 15 miles an hour. A further five years on Stephenson's vehicle was renamed the "Rocket." with the title of "Rocket," took first place in a race which ran all the way from Liverpool until Manchester station. The car broke all records at 37 miles at 36 mph.

At the time canal businesses, compelled to compete in the emerging transport industry, cut their rates, but luckily for them they were not the only ones to suffer. The railway industry was already making waves and was able to make a mark on people. Growing demand for railways led to"railway mania "railway mania" from 1844-1848 In the nineteenth century, officials were no longer able to ignore the demands of the people to an overhaul.

The saying goes that the change has to come from within. This is what happened to Robert Owen, who inherited an old cotton mill in the year the year 1800 in New Lanark, rose to the heights of. The mill was founded fifteen years earlier by his father and another well-known person, Richard Arkwright, was the most modern facility it could be. But when Owen took a look at his mighty staff of 2500 people, the uninitiated young mill owner was horrified by the horrible living conditions the staff had to work and live in. Intoxication and criminality were rampant in the nearby community of New Lanark Mill, but the reason for this, Owen believed, was caused by the ill-will that were brought on by the inhumane, blood-sucking factories. Therefore, Owen decided to set an example for others by changing the process. The entire cotton mill and accommodation facilities for employees were updated from the top to the bottom. Owen increased the wages of staff, however, he kept the cost of the village stores unchanged, thus sacrificing the firm's profits that were once a soaring margin. Owen also offered the opportunity to receive scholarships, a low-cost education as well as health insurance to people living in New Lanark. New Lanark community. Owen's success with his innovative business model proved the concept of ethics as well as financial success could be a balanced combination that was feasible to attain.

Owen

Owen's goodwill in the past helped open the doors to the reforms which followed. In 1802, the Parliament passed the Health and Morals of Apprentices Act which reduced working hours down from 14 hours to a maximum of 12 per day. After that, there was the release of the Sadler Report in 1833, that was a set of hearings centered around the conclusions of Michael Sadler's investigation into the cruel and unorthodox child labor.

Based on Sadler's interview with 89 children who were working It was found that kids even as young as age 8 did not get a break from 11-12 hours of work. One boy in the age of Peter Smart testified that children were kept in the factory throughout the night to keep escape attempts at times. Following one of his unsuccessful escape attempts, he was taken back into the loft of the master and "thrashed with a whip."

Elizabeth Bentley of Leeds, aged 23 also shared her personal story. She was just 6 years old less than many of us, and she joined work as doffer (one who was able to replace Bobbins) as well as an errand runner. for a period of about a year she was forced to do 16-hour shifts starting at 5 am and going until 9 pm in the evening. It was no surprise that Bentley and other kids, could barely get their tired bodies out of their beds. Naturally, this resulted in a strapping as well as, at times it was a dock on their wages.

Sadler's Report led to the publication of the Factory Act that same year. While children were still not completely removed from working in the manner that Sadler was planning however, their hours of work were subject to some snatching. The children between 9 to 16 were only allowed to work for eight hours as well as being forced to attend school two hours every weekday. The cost of tuition was to be borne by the school's teacher.

In 1834 In 1834, the Poor Law Amendment ordered the building of houses for the poor that would be constructed for those poor in the community. In 1842 the Mines Act banned women, along with children below 10 years old from work in mines as well as other industries related to it. A year after, an amendment to the Factory Act that was issued decreased the work hours for women and children working in textile mills for children between 8-13 hours to six and a half hours per each day. In addition the children were now given an additional hour of schooling each weekday.

Then came The Ten Hour Act of 1847 that further reduced the hours of work for everyone British females and teens regardless of their profession. Following were further acts which promoted more tolerable work hours, and the significance of education.

The End of an Era

"The Industrial Revolution was another of those extraordinary jumps forward in the story of civilization." Claudio Magris

Whatever the positives and negatives, Britain had become one of the most vibrant and powerful industrial powers across the globe. Around 1835, 106,000 power looms had been installed all over the world in 1890. By that time there was a claim that 90% of the ships around the globe were built in Britain. The year 1852 was when the wonderful country reached a new landmark, with over 7700 miles of railway tracks that ran through the nation.

More structural reforms were implemented throughout the 19th century as a way to enhance the management and policing of every industry and society in general. In 1848, Parliament set up the General Board of Health, an organization charged with overseeing the oversight and enforcement of hygiene standards throughout Britain and industries across the globe. Additionally, separate boards were established in towns, cities, and parishes, to monitor the cleanliness of drinking water.

Through the Public Health Act of 1875 and the Public Health Act of 1875, the British government was pledging to ensure the management and quality control needed in the sewage and housing system. Then in 1901, another change of the Factory Act bumped up the threshold for entry into factory workers from 12 to 12. The legislature then decided to put the focus of reforming the system of education. A second amendment to the Education Act declared school a compulsory requirement for children from 10 years old as well as 38 years after, until the age of 14.

In 1944 The bar was raised yet again, this time to 18 inches. At this point, it was when Britain's Industrial Revolution in Britain finally was drawing towards a conclusion. It was home to two thirds of the world's coke and 50% of the world's production of iron.

It is impossible to better describe all the glory of the Industrial Revolution than the Great Exhibition of the Works of Industry of All Nations, that opened its doors to the public on 1st of May, 1851. Tourists from both near and far gathered in Omnibuses, which rolled through the pulsating, meandering avenues of Knightsbridge as well as towards Hyde Park. There was the royal palace constructed from gleaming cast iron with the glass-like exterior shimmering under the golden glow from the sunlight. The London palace, also known by its name, The Crystal Palace, would be the perfect location for what was to be referred to as the world's first fair.

Modern depictions from the Great Exhibition

The palace's interior impressed visitors. The doors to this magnificent building were 100,000 of the most dazzling gadgets, gadgets as well as magnificent machines displayed through more than 15,000 fascinating display shows. The carpeted, lush flooring of the gallery upstairs were bathed in the colorful light that poured through the colorful stained-glass windows. The gallery was also the host and half the gallery was used for British artifacts.

One of the most striking aspects that was on display was the Robert Stevenson's massive hydraulic press. This was the one which was employed to raise the steel tubes that made up a bridge in Bangor. Visitors had never before seen something like this before - every one tube must have been weighing 1,144 tons however it required more than one person to operate the presses. It was equally mind-blowing to see a steam-hammer that was just a couple of exhibitions away. It was believed to be strong enough to create the bridges' bearings as well as steamships and buildings yet at the same it was also equipped with the grace and gentleness to gently make an egg loose. The other exhibit featured a revolutionary printer that was able to print thousands of copies within an hour.

In the following five months, more than six million people walked through the barrier, from where they were able to wander freely around the amusement park with industrial wonders. Every section was marked with flags, banners as well as other iconic objects that best represented the country's history. The exhibit featured pianos that fold perfect for sailors as well as those traveling. Also, there was the machine that created fresh rolled cigarettes. A display showcased "tangible ink" for the blind. Another showcased "sportsman knives" equipped with the capacity of 80 knives. Also captivating was a gallery with amazing cars, wagons, as well as various other forms of transportation with all kinds of shapes and sizes. It was, for absence of a better term truly amazing.

In the hall of exhibits, people were spellbound and were surrounded by things that would soon revolutionize the world and bring the world into the time of technological advancement.

Chapter 7: The Pre-Revolution

If you encounter the term "revolution," the first thought that pops into their mind is a political uprising that is of some sort. The word "revolution" has numerous meanings. Revolt is the term used to describe dissociation from something usually a type of the government. When you add an "ing" and it becomes an adjective that means some thing that is disgusting. It could be also a verb, an act of putting on the act of retaliation.

"Revolution" can also mean that you complete a circle, to turn around or roll back. It's a bit odd that the word "revolution" can also refer to anything that is deemed to be extraordinary, the advancement of something or even before its time, for instance the case of a breakthrough development.

It's this last point which most accurately describes what we call the Industrial Revolution. Klaus Schwab, a German engineer and economist, articulated it beautifully when he described an revolution to be "the appearance of new technologies and novel ways of perceiving the world [that] trigger a profound change in economic and social structures." 1. Actually Schwab thinks we're entering"the" Fourth Industrial Revolution. This is a shocking thought for many because they aren't aware that there has been many.

Farm girl making butter.

Prior to industrialization the entire process was performed with a hand. As we consider the beginning of the 1800s and prior to the advent of technology, in comparison to how the present the way things were done was difficult to do, which was time-consuming and labour-intensive. Clothing was made of skins, or fabric that was created by hand and then put together using a hand. The fields were ploughed by using animals for power. Milking cows was done by hand and butter was churned with hands, (taking about 30 minutes to churn continuously).

Every thing is on the market currently that's manufactured with machines was made originally manually.

The majority of historians agree that the agriculture revolution was the pivotal incident that led to an industrial revolution. This is so much that, if it wasn't for it, history could be completely different.

Farming

From the early 1800's onwards Farmers would plant identical crops in the same areas each year. They understood that if soil was not allowed to "rest," the quality of the crop decreased in time, as substances like nitrogen (more required for some crop types than for others) getting diminished.

In 1730 In the 1730s, in the 1730s, a British statesman by the name Charles Townsend was the first to advocate the idea of rotation in the crop. Through the cultivation of different crops on their fields, year after year, farmers can preserve the soil's quality and never need to let their fields remain in a state of negligence. Townsend suggested farmers plant an agricultural crop, and then in the next, grow an edible crop would be grown in the field. Since he proposed turnips as a possible vegetable crop (a important ingredient in roots cellars at the time), Townsend became known as "Turnip Townsend." 2.

This new way of agriculture increased amount of food available in Britain. Food supply increased, which meant healthier as well, which led to a rise in population because of it. Population growth would be crucial in the period of industrial revolution since the equipment required to power the revolution demanded an increased number of workers to run and keep running.

New methods of agriculture that revolutionized the world needed revolutionary machinery to help these new methods. One machine that had significant impact on the revolution in agriculture was the seed drill developed by a man called Jethro Tull.

Jethro Tull, born 1674.

Tull was born in Berkshire, England in 1674 in a family of wealth. Because of this being educated, he had a good education and planned to pursue an upcoming career in politics, but an illness slowed his plans. He was married in 1699 possibly due to because of the desire to support his family and wife they hoped to provide for that led him to go back to his family and joined with his father at the farm that was owned by his parents. All work was performed with a hand and the methods for planting did not differ - seeds were planted manually in neat rows. They were also made by animal and human energy. In recognizing this as efficient, Tull created a drill that rotated to cultivate the seeds. The process was made easier and faster, without wasting any time. But, many farmers weren't ready to accept this approach since they were firmly rooted that they were still using the traditional methods of farming.

The seed drill of Tull.

Incredibly convinced that he had invented a revolutionary technology, Tull traveled to Europe to study more about seed cultivation and the agricultural system in general. Based on European agriculture practices He learned about the best size of the seed to be planted and the distance they ought to be for maximum development. Also, he learned that planting straight rows reduced space, which allowed farmers to utilize less seeds, making more efficient weeding. In Europe the farmer also invented an innovative plough which would enable farmers to plant similar crop in the same area in consecutive seasons.

Through his quest to learn, Tull came to the conclusion that soil was the sole food source the plants required, however it needed to be the right. The book Horse-Hoeing Husbandry, he writes "Too much nitre (or other salts) corrodes a plant; too much water drowns it; too much air dries the roots of it; too much heat (or fire) burns it; but too much earth a plant can never have, unless it be therein wholly buried... Too much earth, or too fine can never possibly be given to roots, for they never receive so much of it as to surfeit the plant." (Surfeit refers to an excess quantity of something.)

Learning from his experiences and the need to share his knowledge resulted in him writing the publication Pasture of Plants. The book states "That that nourishes and enhances an organism is the actual nutrition of it. All plants are earth growing and the real expansion of a plant comes from an increase in the amount of earth."

Farmers began to realize the increasing efficiency of Tull's techniques and eventually embraced them. Tull as well as Townsend together are believed to be responsible for the revolution in agriculture which soon was sweeping across Britain as well as Europe and led to the beginning of the industrial revolution. Since fewer people needed to cultivate the land there was a rise in idle people moved to cities.

Commerce

In addition to the agricultural revolution the historians have also pointed to different events or modifications in the ideology of trade that contributed into the Industrial Revolution. In the mix is the rise of a modern model of capitalism.

Before the Industrial Revolution The transfer of funds was regulated by monarchies. Mercantilism or mercantilism, as it was known as, was managed by government which had a strict supervision and regulations. Economic thinkers who were free of regulations such as Adam Smith Scottish author and economics expert Adam Smith began to promote new ways of thinking. One which favored more liberty for people.

In his novel The Wealth of Nations, Smith opposed government control of the economy as well as mercantilism, in favor of what he termed "the invisible hand." This referred to the purest version of capitalism in which the forces of market demand and supply are driving forces in the economy. Smith believed that capitalism is responsible for the revolution in industrialization because industrialization was triggered and controlled by the populace rather than the state. In Britain when the revolution started wealthy investors were able to create factories and build mining sites to supply the equipment needed to manage the revolution.

Inspiring only by the promise of the prospect of profit (and possibly in the name of greed) and possibly greed, the revolution would be impossible without the advent of the capitalist system, and at that period was referred to as "laissez-faire capitalism." Also known as "free market" or just "market" capitalism, the words refer to the notion that government officials should remain from the field of economics, and let individuals pursue their interests without being weighed down by a myriad of laws and laws. Laissez-faire means "leave us alone."

Another element that contributed to the revolution in industrial production was the expansion of European imperialism. "European imperialism was vital to the start of the Industrial Revolution (especially in Britain)." 3 The term "imperialism" refers to the rule of a nation or region over the other by military, political or economic power. The 1700s saw the expansion of trade in Britain, with those from France, Spain, Belgium, Germany, and other European nations, was establishing significant control over Africa, China, North and South America, India and Australia. In the Age of Imperialism, the nations in power had the final say on the goods that were provided to their partners in trade. The European countries looked after one another and made sure that each was supplied with the right supply and routes to trade set up to help aid their economies and expand by colonization of other countries.

In this period it was when during this time, the Trade Triangle was formed. This comprised Europe, Africa and the Americas, Europe and Africa which allowed European traders to move their merchandise across existing trade routes. The trade also made slavery of slaves who were transported from central Africa across Africa to the Americas for sale (at high profit and adding to the European as well as the British economic growth) then put to work in plantations. European traders would then bring the plantations' raw materials the plantations returning to Europe as well as Britain to be processed at their factories. In the course of time, the Trade Triangle became responsible for transporting the raw materials, individuals, as well as manufactured goods back and forward through the Atlantic Ocean.

When it became apparent the possibility of replacing manpower with machines, the necessity for fuel was a key aspect in the first stages of the revolutionary era. The coal reserves of Britain was the main source of power in the period prior to the beginning stages of the revolution. In contrast to Europe it was located close to the surface and cheaper to mine. This made the money toward the development of factories as well as purchasing products that came from trade routes like the Trade Triangle. Steam engines became essential to the extraction of coal.

Chapter 8: The First Industrial Revolution

As one of the biggest ever recorded in the history of mankind time, the beginning of the industrial revolution is believed as having begun at the time of Great Britain in the mid-1750s from 1760 and continued until about 1830. The revolution began with, what we call as agriculture. It was the change from an agricultural and craft-based society which was dominated by manufacturing and industry machines. Through the implementation of the Townsend's better program for crop rotation and the Tull seed driver and plough farmers could decrease their cost of production since less effort was needed as well as less raw materials required due to the increased effectiveness.

Thanks to this improved efficiency, lesser labor was needed for more production farms, so farmers quit their farms to seek higher incomes to provide for their families and boost their buying power. The influx of workers created a large and consistent pool of employees that could fuel the new industrial. The banks that were already in place embraced this new trend (and the new capitalism of laissez-faire) and aided in financing the development of new manufacturing and industry. Industry-focused entrepreneurs wanted to be part of this latest development in wealth that they believed to be the opportunity which would lead to a better future. Commerce was the new gold band.

The industrialists were becoming wealthy as those who had gone to farms with hopes of higher wages and, consequently living a better lifestyle, turned into metaphorical slaves to the rich - shipowners and merchants were the mainstay of the newly prosperous. People of the working class was in poverty in cramped environments and had no comforts. Women were given different roles after leaving working in the fields to work in textile industries and even as domestic aid. Payed just enough to pay the essential expenses for food and shelter family members had to take their kids to with the cost of living. When they were enlisted to work in factories, they were required endure long working shifts and earned only a tiny fraction of the amount their parents earned.

Children's labor was particularly appealing for the wealthy factory owners. Since they only received 10-20 % of the wages earned by their parents and thus, employing them could save the business owners money. They were also discovered to be submissive to adults, with less complaints and resolving disputes quietly. (For example, in factories floor supervisors were instructed to whip workers who weren't on time for reporting - this that included children.)

Textiles

Children are a key benefit in making textiles because of their tiny and agile fingers, which could be able to fit comfortably into the work of a spinning frame that was jammed.

The Spinning Jenny.

In 1764 In 1764, in 1764, the Spinning Jenny was invented by John Hargreaves, a British weaver, carpenter and inventor. Since multiple spindles moved extremely quickly The Jenny could create yarn much faster and at greater volumes that in a hand spinner.

But, it was not uncommon for the yarn to got stuck, and the children's smaller and less agile fingers could easily free themselves from the blockage, but often they got hurt during the process.

Cotton would become an important player in the time of the revolution in Britain. At the beginning of the 17th century Britain was renowned for its woolen-woven fabric and worsted fabrics. Even today the woolens from any place within the British Isles are coveted.

The beginning of making cloth was a lengthy and tedious job. In order to spin, wool has been sorted. This can be done with two paddles, both of which is covered with rows of extremely small and thin steel teeth. Wool is loaded in two layers on one carder, by pulling pieces out of an assemblage. One hand is placed over the clump of wool on the carder, another is gently pulled back, leaving a layer over the teeth of the carder, the process repeats until you have two equal layers.

Making a rolag with hand-held cards.

Utilizing very soft strokes and beginning with the loose ends of the wool. One will then take the carder and teeth it down and gently brushes the wool fibers that were gathered that were combed by the first. The strands are separated to ensure that, when done the wool is left as a piece of wool that has been combed, known as a rolag. The spinner then creates threads that are used to make weaving and warp.

In the past there were three carders to supply enough rolags one spinner to be engaged as well as three spinners to give enough yarn to a weaver to make cloth. This was a process that involved everyone in the family, and was non-biased as both women and men performed all of the tasks as well as the kids in the household. It was usually the sole source of income aside from the meager crop that would be grown at the farm of the family and leftovers after having fed all the family members.

If the weaver isn't using his own wool a weaver on a handloom would go to homes of his neighbors to collect any remaining weft that they may possess, the weft being spun yarn which is then being threaded between the warp by an armature into which yarn is passed through. The warp yarn is stretched before being woven onto the loom. It remains in place. Because it's stretched onto the loom, it needs to be more durable than weft. After the weaver had got the weft into his loom and brought it back, prepare it for loading onto the shuttle and then begin weaving.

The Industrial Revolution profoundly altered the way people lived. The children were employed in textile mills for a multitude of years. A particular mill was 100 people busy. more than half of them suffering injuries of a variety. Many times, hand and arms of children were entangled in machines "in many instances the muscles, and the skin is stripped down to the bone, and in some instances a finger or two might be lost". 4 In light of the laissez-faire approach to business intervention by the state injuries, the victims were frequently removed from the working force, and often abandoned, especially youngsters. Companies weren't obliged to assume the responsibility for injuries to employees' medical needs as well as compensation for rehabilitation. This was an extremely difficult time for workers.

Although still something we'd call barbaric today the child labor laws that were passed in Britain during the 1800s helped make things more palatable. They were known as"the Factory Acts, they established that kids under nine years of age weren't allowed to be employed, while those aged 9 to 16 were allowed to be employed "only" 16 hours a per day. It was the Cotton Mills Act, put in place in 1856 let children who were over nine years old to be employed for a maximum of 60 hours a week, all day and evening.

In the wake of their popularity textiles were among the first to benefit from the new era. These factories employed the largest number of individuals and offered the highest returns on investment. The textile industry was among the first to utilize what at the day of time was deemed to be the most modern methods of production following Jethro Tull's invention of a sewer (which was still requiring a man and woman pushing it into the earth).

In 1784 In 1784, an English inventor with the name of Edmund Cartwright designed a prototype of a power loom made from paper. The first model was constructed in 1785, and was later to undergo numerous iterations. It was a long time of testing and experimenting before the loom could be thought to be fully automated. In 1850, there were around 260,000 looms operating throughout England. In the end, the loom improved to be able to replenish the shuttle whenever it became empty. The loom was referred to as the Northrop Loom which later changed to an automated Lancashire Loom.

Mill engine operating in a bobbin mill.

The Steam Engine

After the advances in the industry of textiles the next big breakthrough in the process was utilizing the invention which actually predated the revolution by about fifty years. The invention that was made included the steam motor. Steam-driven engines were already operating in the early century AD The first operational steam engine was developed by Thomas Newcomen in 1712.

Steam engines are combustion engines that operate externally. The steam pressure creates an internal combustion engine that turns a piston in the cylindrical. The force generated by the motion of the piston gets transfered to a rod and flywheel. This creates a rotating force. This force of rotation that drives the engine.

The latest model to the Watt dual-acting steam engine.

In Newcomen's initial working model the steam was permitted to escape. James Watt made a substantial enhancement to the design of Newcomen in 1776. He seized steam, and directing it to be used in a different engine. The result was known in Watt Steam Engine, or the Watt Steam Engine, or the Boulton and Watt steam engine. The latter was which included Watt's co-worker Matthew Boulton. The steam engine was vital power source in order for factories to boost production as well as to aid in shipping goods through steamships as well as railway.

Mining

Iron ore was an essential element in the beginning of the industrial revolution. Mining was a huge and expensive business. Thanks to steam engines it was possible to draw water from the mines rapidly and more efficiently. Before the Revolution, Britain was dependent on charcoal as cheap and readily available fuel. It was readily available through two types of mines - drift mines and bell pits. But both of them produced tiny quantities of coal enough to supply the requirements of the population as well as small-scale industry of the day. With the growth of population and production increased and the demand for power grew with it. Mines for coal had to travel deeper in order to extract greater coal and the job became more hazardous. The children were employed in the mines since they were able to squeeze in the small shafts of mine as well as assist in moving coal from the bottom to the top.

Miner

Mine shafts could extend several hundred feet deep into the earth. The water had to be pumped out and toxic gas (such like carbon monoxide) could pose a serious threat. The method of sending the canary in a mine before miners in order to look for poisonous gasses did not start before 1911. Prior to this mining, miners didn't have any way to know if they were in an unintentional death trap. An explosion always possible. An ignition from the pickaxe of a miner could light the gas-filled tunnel that would then impose the actual burden of earth over the miner's crew. Canaries were used for mining continued up to 1986.

Like we said, the working conditions in Britain during the time of the revolution were abysmal. This led to a rise in frustration among workers increased and English workers in the textile industry formed a secret group known as the Luddites. For membership the Luddites, you must take an oath in support of their ideas that were founded upon the notion that technology could be used to circumvent standard working procedures. In Orson Wells' 1984 book, released in 1949, people were scared that they would become machines (as they are still doing in the present). In 1811 In 1811, the Luddites protested in a number of the factories in England by smashing up their machines that they had feared. Today, the word "luddite" has come to refer to anyone who is opposed to technological advancement, including computers (technology) or automation and other advanced technologies. As a result of the Luddite protests and general anger of the working class early trade unions were legally recognized in Britain in 1824.

Luddite leader.

The Spread of the Revolution

The Revolution was slow to propagate throughout Great Britain to Europe and beyond because of the restrictions set by Brits. They knew they were ahead of the pack in the manufacture of cotton and wool (wool as well as cotton) as well as machinery and equipment, they held a massive advantage when it came to getting into markets that demanded the products. There was no one else to meet the demands which is why they banned exports of machines or skilled labour, as well as the sharing of manufacturing methods. Their advantage was not going to last forever.

Belgium was the first country in Europe to implement the modern technology and machines. In search of a commercial opportunity Two Englishmen set up machines at Liege, Belgium. Coal, iron, as well as textiles were their top industry.

France was slow to adopt modern industrial practices, partly because of being a part of the French Revolution occurring at the exact as the French Revolution (1787-1799). It was the country's wealth that was utilized to finance the Revolution and the investors weren't keen to invest in industrial advancements within a volatile world of politics.

Germany was not quick to embrace new strategies because of political turmoil. The only time national unification was reached around 1870 that the country began to develop industrialization. After the process began However, Germany quickly beat Britain when it came to the manufacturing of steel. They also managed to be a global top chemical manufacturing company.

Cotton

The creation of the Trade Triangle and the development of steam engines to propel ships across the Atlantic brought the revolutionary era in America. United States. When the technology of weaving looms to produce thread and yarn advanced as did the demand for cotton material grew. As slaves were regularly transported into in the United States to work on the farms, cotton farmers realized that they were growing an "cash cow" crop - should a better method was found to eliminate seeds, other than manually.

Eli Whitney faced a series of circumstances that brought him to Georgia following the passing of her mother; the demonstrations by his stepmother in opposition to going to college, his being a teacher in a public school, finding it difficult to finance his plans to go to law school, and finally accepting an offer to be tutoring for private students at a private school in South Carolina. Eli Whitney was able to sail with fellow New Englanders looking for fortunes in the South. One of them were Catherine Littlefield Greene and her family. The widow was of Revolutionary War hero General Nathanael Greene from Rhode Island. Catherine was able to convince Whitney to travel to her farm located in Georgia, Mulberry Grove, to pay a visit instead of South Carolina. Catherine's husband after her, Phineas Miller, also from New England, would become an important figure to Whitney's life.

Eli was the inventor. While working at Mulberry Grove Eli came up with a variety of innovative devices that could be utilized in the home. Eli so was awed Catherine by his innovations that she introduced him the business community who were who were interested in creating a device which could separate the seeds from the shorter growing cotton fields in the uplands across the South. The work that was done manually produced only 1 pound of pure cotton per day per employee. They called Whitney to check whether he could find the best way to do it.

It only took him two weeks to come up with his idea of the cotton gin, which is the short form for engine. Much like the paddles employed to sew cotton the gin consisted of nothing other than a stick of wood equipped with hooks to pull cotton into an extremely thin mesh. The cotton seeds, which were too large for the net, could drop out to the side. Production increased from one per day of a pound (per worker) to 55 pounds a day of clean cotton with only one cotton gin.

The gin is on display in the Eli Whitney Museum in Hamden, Connecticut.

Miller Catherine's husband, who was her new was Whitney's business partner. Their idea was to provide the cleaning service for farmer's cotton plantation instead of selling them a single of the cotton Gins. The basis of the currency was cotton. People who owned the plantation resented this because they were required give up two-fifths the value of each plant that was removed. Even though Whitney received an patent for his device but the laws regarding patents were loose and eventually, the other manufacturers saw the lucrative potential, and made similar machines, which they offered to plantation owners.

Whitney and Miller were unable to keep pace with the market, and were eventually out-sold by other manufacturers. The company went out of business just three years after the Gin was created.

The story is that Whitney's style had issues, as is normal for the first time. There is a rumor that the person who suggested solutions to the shortcomings was the none less than Catherine Greene, who had been Whitney's initial partner. Whitney didn't give her acknowledgment of her work. Despite its shortcomings it is thought to have changed southern agriculture's business and revived slavery. The cotton industry became the main export in the United States between 1820 and the year 1860.

The remarkable inventions kept coming throughout the industrial revolution as it was progressing. The increased production led to the necessity to expand transportation options and improved communication to bring goods into the marketplace. Railways didn't exist yet. People who had an eye on the future started looking into rivers as transport routes not just for trade but for just getting from one place to another. The first steamboat that was commercially profitable operation was invented through Robert Fulton in 1807. Together with Robert Livingston, they launched the North River Steamboat which was later called Clermont. The steamboat transported people all the way between New York City and the capital of the state, Albany, on the Hudson River. The 150-mile voyage was finished within 32 hours.

Fulton was a lover of steam and boats since his the age of a child. Engineering school was a great help when Fulton designed tugboat canals as well as the first submersible powered by muscles (the Nautilus) and the contemporary torpedo (at that moment). His last creation was the first steam-powered warship.

With the growth of production and trade and a growing large population requiring a faster way to travel increasing the number of transport routes became apparent. The expansion was required if needs for transportation were to be fulfilled. It was necessary to expand the Great Lakes provided a huge river, but it was not an connection other than across the land, and in the majority of cases they had no connectivity. Access was a problem for merchants who wanted to bring their products from Britain and from the east coastline from the United States inland in an efficient method.

Map of the Erie Canal in 1840.

To expand the use of the Hudson River and possible routes that could be utilized for a route to take from New York to the Great Lakes Engineers devised plans and, after the first plan was rejected the construction of what was to be the Erie Canal began in 1817. In 1825, it was complete. canal connected 363 miles of to the Hudson River in Albany (connecting New York City and its ports) and eventually to Lake Ontario and Lake Erie. Merchants and travelers did not have to depend on mules that could pack their products, which were restricted to a maximum weight of 250 pounds cargo or painful stagescoaches to travel between locations.

Grain

Grain was the most important item produced by the Ohio River Valley.

Farmers were able to grow the oats and wheat in huge amounts, but the profit was not that great considering the amount of time and funds required for harvesting. The canal had a positive effect on profits because of the speedier transport process as well as the capability to transport more weight, but profits were very low.

A typical American grain cranny.

The harvesting process was usually performed by hand with the "cradle" or a what could be called an scythe with multiple blades. With a swiveling motion the cradler one who was holding the cradle is known as was a farmer who walked through fields cutting through the wheat shafts. The cradler was accompanied by other workers who bundled and wrapped the wheat with strands of wheat to form tied. They then placed the bundles on the fields and left to dry. The process was a long and time-consuming procedure even though a crane could be able to cover 1.5 to two acres over the course of a day.

Growing in a family farm, the youngest of eight children Cyrus McCormick helped his father with the work of his father in the fields, the same as all kids, today and in the past living on farms. Robert McCormick was an inventor and believed that there was a way to go past hand-harvesting to alternatively use a robotic reaper. Over the course of 28 years, he was working on design after design for a mechanical reaper that was pulled by horses and was not able to build a functioning prototype.

Cyrus McCormick

Cyrus recognized the potential and embraced the idea following the death of his father. He was assisted by Jo Anderson, one of the slaves of McCormick farm, Cyrus also saw the potential. McCormick farm, he designed and developed a device which was powered through horses (in contrast to the Scottish device that was pulled with horses). Though he had numerous successful demonstrations and received an patent in 1834, until 1841, he had failed to make even one. It was later observed, was not able to cope with the different circumstances.

A model from 1845 of McCormick reaper. McCormick reaper.

Through perseverance, Cyrus continued to refine his style. In 1842, he sold seven machines, and due to the success of his product and word-of-mouth marketing his sales continued to grow each year. Together with his brother Cyrus later relocated from Virginia to Chicago in 1842 from Virginia and opened a plant in the city to manufacture his mechanical reaper. It was originally named Cyrus H. McCormick and Brothers however, it was later transformed to McCormick Harvesting Machine Company. Around 1860, more than 100,000 reapers were dispersed[5] and they were shifting the way farming was known.

McCormick Harvesting went through the typical stresses of a firm, which included a court contest regarding patent infringement. The plant was destroyed in 1871 during the Great Chicago Fire of 1871 However, it was the same determination, which led Cyrus to develop his first commercially successful product as well as the encouragement of his wife Cyrus along with his siblings reconstructed the facility. Then, in 1902, his original firm was renamed to be

International Harvester Company. International Harvester Company.

The first industrial revolution was about to come to an final stage, there was further invention that could have a significant influence on agriculture as McCormick's reaper. Plowing in the past was accomplished by hand using an iron blade. Anyone who's had the pleasure of cooking with cast iron cookware knows the strain they put on them. Imagine moving a plow by all the force of a large bent blade of cast iron! The blade was not just massive, but soil would adhere to the mouldboard (the blade) while it moved and turned the soil. In the end, farmers had take a break every couple of minutes to remove the blade. As the settlements grew further away from the east coast, the soil got heavy and the task was becoming more and more laborious.

In the absence of enough businesses in Vermont to sustain itself and thrive, a blacksmith under his name John Deere headed west in the hope of locating a larger number of people to help him with his work. Deere was able to settle outside of Chicago and since there was no blacksmith within 40 miles his company quickly started to flourish. He heard from farmers and learned that plowing was an effort because of the heavy, thicker soil of the Midwest. In most cases, it took 8 yokes of oxen in order to push the plow across the field.

While visiting one of the sawmills in town, Deere spotted a broken steel saw. He brought it to his own workshop, and then shaped it into the blade of a plow. Tests showed that the new blade had a far superior performance in being able to move through soil compared to those made from cast iron. It was in the beginning of 1838 that Deere made two more plowing machines. It was 1838. He was selling and building 75 to 100 Plows per year. [6]

From the blacksmith's trade to a manufacturer, Deere acquired two partners and relocated the business into Moline, Illinois, about 160 miles to the to the west of Chicago. The process was not easy to farmers who were locked with their old ways, as hard to believe, however, with his business acumen tried, Deere slowly garnered the trust required to expand his company. In the present it is the John Deere Company has become the most well-known brand for the entire range of agricultural equipment. The headquarters of the company is located in Moline, Illinois, with an area of 1400 acres. John is likely to be somewhat awestruck by the growth of his family's humble roots in Vermont.

Chapter 9: The Second Industrial Revolution

- Technology Blooms 1870-1914 -

The second wave of industrialization was defined by the use of synthetic materials, such as metallic alloys, lighter metals (for instance, the development of new types of steel) along with plastics, as well as the development of new sources of energy - specifically the invention of electricity. This was also an industrial revolution which led to the development of the very first automated factories.

The ownership of factories or companies was also altered. Although individual ownership was certainly maintained in some measure however, the ownership of companies and facilities shifted from individuals to stockholders and insurance corporations.

The business world's political landscape have also shifted. Prior to the laissez-faire policy that were characterized as "hands off" by government became gradually replaced by rules as the industrialized societies grew increasingly complex.

The time frame for this second revolution started and concluded, however the general consensus is that it should start around 1840. The conclusion of this revolution generally accepted to be at the beginning in World War I, in 1914.

Steel

The steel metal became the material preferred, replacing more heavy and older cast iron. Used in the construction of buildings, railways as well as industrial machinery and ships, steel was less expensive than iron, and reduced the price of manufacturing. Steel enabled faster expansion of railway lines and more efficient transport methods.

The manufacturing process was improved and standardized. The Bessemer Method of making steel was popular because it provided a cost-effective method to produce massive quantities of the metal which was necessary in order to keep pace with the industrialization process.

The Bessemer convertor.

Sir Henry Bessemer applied for the first patent on the process in 1854 although there was some debate over the fact that it was Bessemer or American William Kelly, who actually came up with the idea initially. Bessemer tried to increase the performance of steel to be used in weapons.

His method began with unrefined ferrous pig, stored in the Bessemer converter. The impurities were eliminated from the iron through blowing air into the molten metal and causing it to oxidize. In the beginning it was difficult to get temperatures that were just right. At first, the produced metal was brittle. Owners of the initial four licenses to employ the process patented by him ended up and suing him, alleging that the resultant steel wasn't suitable for cold or hot. The licenses were returned to him by paying a higher price to receive the licenses back than their original purchase price.

Bessemer was aware of the issue on the impurities present found in iron pig. The trick to getting rid of the impurities was to know which time to shut off the flow of air, and burning off the impurities, leaving the proper amount carbon-based alloy. He was able to accomplish it, but was unable to communicate the process to the patent holders. 7 After quitting this method, Bessemer decided to establish his own business of steel production that eventually was one of the biggest companies in the world. This process changed forever how steel was produced.

Henry Bessemer.

When the second revolution began to spread all over America, United States, investors were looking to invest. Steel was one of the most important components within the industry, being employed in almost every phase of production, from factories from the factory to components to railways. American investors were well-aware of changes in UK as well as Europe as well, and some began to inquire about permission to employ Bessemer's process within the US. The first permit to utilize the method was issued in 1863, and was it was granted to two iron manufacturers from New York.

With the mill becoming increasingly productive it attracted new investors to it, among them was that was the Pennsylvania Railroad Company, who was looking to utilize steel for the rails they use. The second mill was constructed to handle this expansion and nine more were to be built in the future. Between 1866-1877, eleven steel mills were operational with the Bessemer process.

Andrew Carnegie, 1913.

Andrew Carnegie became a key investor when he realized the mills as the ideal complement to his previous businesses that comprised Keystone Bridge

Company, Keystone Bridge Company and the Union Ironworks. Carnegie engaged one of the first mill builders to construct him another manufacturing facility for steel and they worked together for a while to refine the manufacturing process. By utilizing Pennsylvania Railroad as a customer Pennsylvania Railroad as a customer and the Bessemer procedure, Carnegie was able to lower the cost of manufacturing steel railways in the half from $100/ton down to just $50/ton. In the 1890s Carnegie was selling steel at just $18/ton. Then he became one of the most well-known industrialists, philanthropists and the richest people in history.

Electricity

Before the widespread usage of electricity, houses factories, houses, and other construction sites were illuminated by candles or gas lamps. In the end, a lot of tasks, like running factories, was done at night to conserve the cost. Electricity revolutionized the way people worked and transformed the way that people did work and lives. The first electricity generators were invented in the early 1870s. Britain was always on top of its game and the first to build an electric power plant for the public in 1881. In 1910, scientists and engineers were able to power an entire urban area with only one power plant.

Since the invention of electricity, incredible things were possible. What exactly is electricity? In simplest terms it's the presence and movement of particles which generate or have an electrical charge. Lightning is a prime example.

Most people attribute Thomas Edison or Benjamin Franklin as being the creators of the bulb light, or the first man to "harness" electricity, but they are not entirely correct. Both of them contributed significantly to the industrial revolution that followed. In particular, Franklin was an inspired inventor and was responsible for the creation of the lightning rod. It all was the result of his famous kite test.

The goal of his experiment was to record or even show the power of electricity in lightning. In order to conduct the test, he required an occurrence of lightning. He was waiting for the right moment to build his kite from silk. It included a wire at the highest point. It was to function as his "lightning rod." The kite was connected with hemp strings, and at the bottom of it, Franklin attached a silk string. The two strings were used to keep him from getting shocked because wet hemp can be charged, while the shorter silk ends will remain dry. Franklin was inside the shed and held the silk end. The most important element was a key made of metal which was affixed on the hemp. With the help of his son, the kite was launched into the wind.

In the midst of waiting and watching, Franklin was about to declare his research a flop when Franklin noticed the loose ends of hemp string, which were standing up straight as if they were hairs that one's arms get caused by static electrical current.

The year was 1752 and it's unclear if the electric field of human bodies was known at that point however for whatever reason, he noticed hemp's strands erect, Franklin slowly approached the key of iron with his finger. When the electric ions positive generated by his fingers attracted negative particles inside the key, he saw sparks. In order to confirm the cause like many researchers are doing, he became their own experiment guinea-pig, and he touched the key made of metal. It is likely that it was an electric shock.

The story of Franklin's experiments was published in Franklin's own words by the newspaper Pennsylvania Gazette on October 19 1872.

"As when any Thunder Clouds pass on top of the Kite The sharp Wire draws it's Electric Fire from them, and the Kite, along with the entire Twine, will become electrified. any loose particles of Twine will shine in each direction, and will be sucked in to a Finger that's coming towards. When the Rain will have soaked the Kite and the Twine in such a way that it will be able to conduct its Electric Fire freely, you can see it gushing out in a large quantity from the Key at it. Approach on your Knuckle. On the Key the Phial could be charged; in turn, as the Electric Fire thus obtain'd, the Spirits can be ignited as well as all other electric experiments can be carried out, that are typically performed with using the Rubbed Glass Globe or tube as well as the resemblance of The Electric Matter with that of Lightning is clearly demonstrated."

For clarity, however, Franklin wasn't the first to show the presence of electric currents in lightning. In the same month an Frenchman named Thomas-Francois dalibard had demonstrated the same fact.

Franklin continued to work on electricity, and in 1753 was awarded the Copley

Medal from the Royal Society for "his interesting research and observations about electricity."[8[8.]

Reconstruction of Edison's Lab.

Thomas Edison was also famous for his experiments with electricity. However, it was his use of electricity to power devices that made him well-known. A prime example of this is the quadruplex Telegraph Machine, which enabled the simultaneous transmission of four signals. Edison was able to sell the machine and utilized the profits to construct an industrial research laboratory located in New Jersey.

Edison by using the second version of his the phonograph.

The ability to first enjoy private music can be traced back to Edison since Edison was the creator of the phonograph, which was invented in 1878. It's hard to envision that his first recordings were made using the foil of tinfoil that was wrapped around the cylindrical. The foil deteriorated fast and each record could only be played for a couple of times. However, the phonograph made Edison into famous. He was recognized with 1 093 patents.

The second industrial revolution was not without its importance. innovations made in Second Industrial Revolution. The process was completed within the span of 40 years! The use of machines was crucial in the evolution of mass production. As an example, 32,000 machine tools were employed in the development for Model T. Model T car made by Ford and all powered with electricity.

The procedure of making paper became more refined when it became more efficient to extract wood fibers that could be used to create papers and Rags. Imagine a world without paper. Imagine a world with no newspapers or an office that doesn't have stationary. Imagine being unable to take the latest book. The development of paper was a major influence on the society, both economically and socially.

The progress in chemical and petroleum industries. Kerosene lamps were commonly used at home until the 1920s. Synthetic dyes were first introduced to the market in 1922, starting with a dark hue of purple.

Transportation was also evolving. The bicycle and the automobile became popular, but at first the wheels were built out of wire or wood. The 1840s were when an American known as Charles Goodyear developed a process known as vulcanization, which helped to make rubber more durable. This allowed companies to create environmentally sustainable tires made of rubber. They replaced the old wire and wooden ones.

The expression "applied science" became popular in order to define the application of scientific know-how for a specific purpose for example, making use of the scientific method of metal metallurgy produce steel. The understanding of chemistry was crucial to the creation of fertilizers as well as dyes and cooking ingredients.

Telecommunications were influenced in many ways. Alexander Graham Bell patented the first phone in 1876. Prior to this, communications were transferred via cables using the telegraph system, however it was only possible after electricity was discovered and put into use. In the early part century in the early 1900s, the wireless telephone (later to be renamed radio) was invented by the Italian inventor named Guglielmo Marconi. After successfully transmitting the very first wireless communication across open waters between Salisbury Plain in England to Signal Hill, Newfoundland, Canada and then he launched an online subscription service that sent evening news reports to vessels crossing the Atlantic.

Management of business was developed using applied science, namely an analysis of workflow methods - with the aim of improving the efficiency of labor and economic efficiency. It was referred to as "Taylorism" after the man who came up with the idea, Frederick Winslow Taylor. This is also known as "scientific management. The study of motion and time examined the number of steps that required to make the item. Then, Taylor's theories were employed to cut down on those processes. Taylor's techniques are being taught and utilized to this day. The principles he outlined were

• Replacing ways of performing things because they have always been done in this manner using methods that are based on conducting a research investigation of the job.

• Establishing the key selection criteria for employees, their training and personal growth instead of placing anyone in a particular job and then expecting that they learn.

Giving detailed instructions to every employee.

Structure work for workers and managers in a way managers, employing the scientific method of assigning work set out the tasks to be completed, while the employees carried out these strategies.

Anyone who has worked for an employer in a business environment (i.e. that is not self-employed) This may sound quite familiar.

The second revolution caused profound effects on the standard of living for the people living in the midst of it. Between 1870-1890 witnessed the highest growth in economic activity of prior similar periods. The increased productivity brought lower prices and living standards increased.

But, as many believe is the case the rate of unemployment grew as technology replaced the work that were previously performed by men as well as women. It's a typical catch-22 scenario industrialization has led to greater production, more items being sold on the market, improved transport methods for getting the goods on the market as well as business potential for entrepreneurs that had funds. But people who did not have the resources to grow or upgrade were watching their companies fail and their businesses were ruined.

In the areas capable of taking advantage of modern transport routes the failure of crops resulted in starvation. In the introduction of sewer system and the requirement to treat water resulted in greater sanitation and better public health.

Industrial revolution II permanently altered the method by which products were made and also how individuals lived their lives and worked. It also altered the nature of war.

The metallurgical industry improved its manufacturing techniques for stronger steel as well as iron, the weaponry of the war gained. Weapons were more durable. Tanks got tougher. The artillery became more efficient. The principles of physics led applied science to discover new explosives and precise methods for hitting targets. Submarines were improved, and battleships became able to maneuver through the sea better. The advancements in chemistry led to the creation of toxic gases.

The start of World War I marked the conclusion of the second industrial revolution when the entire world invested all of the wisdom gained over the past 40years towards fighting on the home front. The beginning of a new era wouldn't occur until the year 1969.

Chapter 10: The Third Industrial Revolution

- The Digitalization of Life -

The people referred to as the Millennials (or Gen Y) have been born from 1981 and. In their world, having computers is as routine as taking off their shoes. It is hard to imagine the first computers as big as their rooms and that required special training in order to use the machines!

Forbes Magazine interviewed Dr. David Brown in 2015 about the predictions of this expert and his insights on the future of living during the 3rd industrial revolution. The main technologies that would be advanced were communications and the internet and energy as well as finance, financial, as well as medical technology. [9]

Internet

Computers were introduced in the early 1900s for use by government agencies at the beginning to record the census. This was already being conducted as in the 1800s. In the early 1800s, English mathematician Charles Babbage was the first to come up with a concept for the steam-powered computer which would include numbers. The famous mathematician is also infamous for not having built the device.

But, the design later developed in the Museum of Science in London, England, to commemorate the past of computer technology. The machine was controlled by a massive crank, this machine contained 8000 parts, and performed and efficiently. It has a replica displayed in the Silicon Valley Computer Museum in California. Although it was able to just add numbers, it was known as"a "difference engine," Babbage's invention is claimed to be able to handle complicated polynomial equations better than any calculator that is hand-held.

Babbage Difference Engine

It was 1936 in 1936, Alan Turing presented the idea that computers could be able to compute anything that is measured. Then, later dubbed"the" Turing Machine, it became the foundational concept for today's computer systems.

In 1937 physics and mathematics professor from Iowa, J.V. Atanasoff tried, but failed to create the world's first computer with no the use of gears, belts or shafts. He was in 1941 when he along with one of his students from the graduate program, Clifford Berry, designed the first computer with multiple memory.

The year 1943 to 1944, John Mauchly and J. Presper Eckert, two University of Pennsylvania professors, constructed what they called"the Electronic Numerical Integrator and Calculator (ENIAC). It was regarded as the first computer with a digital interface with 18,000 vacuum tubes that filled an area of 20 by 40 feet. It was in 1946 that Mauchly along with Eckert signed in a deal together with the United States Census Bureau to create the first computer that could be used in commercial and government applications.

Through the years over the years, this "language" to operate computers has undergone several changes, starting with COBOL which is the Common Business Oriented Language. Personal computers came on the market in 1974. Made in the name of IBM, Radio Shack, Commodore and Altair in the early years, they may have been in the forefront of technology, but they were not yet widely used at a personal basis. In 1975, two computer geeks who were just beginning their careers proposed to create programs for the Altair making use of the most recent computer programming language called BASIC - that the usage of personal computers grew. The geeks involved included Paul Allen and Bill Gates In 1975 Microsoft came into existence.

In the year 1976, Apple computers was formed during the day of April Fool's Day. In 1977 it was the year that it was the year that Apple II came out at the very first West Coast Computer Fair. The Apple II was the first computer that had color graphics as well as an audio cassette player that was used for storage.

Computers were constantly improving their ability to accomplish what humans could not or at an even faster pace; but, they're only capable of the data you fed them. Thus, the phrase "junk in and junk out, or GIGO which means garbage in and garbage out. At the time, computers were self-contained computers that were able to access data locally, be it through local storage or networks.

Berners-Lee in 2005.

The world changed completely in March of 1989 when a lesser-known British computer scientist and engineer suggested (and created) the term we know as the initial three characters in an internet address. WWW means the World Wide Web. The name of the person is Timothy Berners-Lee.

Employed at the time by CERN, the largest internet node in Europe in the

1980s, he was the first to propose the use of hypertext, a way of communicating between computers to share research information. In his own words, he describes his coup d'état of computer wizardry by saying, "I just had to take the hypertext idea and connect it to the Transmission Control Protocol and domain name system ideas and—ta-da!—the World Wide Web... Creating the web was really an act of desperation, because the situation without it was very difficult when I was working at CERN later. Most of the technology involved in the web, like the hypertext, like the internet, multifont text objects, had all been designed already. I just had to put them together. It was a step of generalising, going to a higher level of abstraction, thinking about all the documentation systems out there as being possibly part of a larger imaginary documentation system."[10]

Once the WWW was created, something that good couldn't help but expand away from strictly government and scientific applications to personal use. Without the capacity to share knowledge as we know it today, computers would simply be faster calculators and a way to store information but not share it.

While we do use the terms interchangeably, the internet is not to the same thing as the World Wide Web, although one depends on the other. The internet, as the name implies, is an interconnected network of computers. Without it, the "web" – the mass of information – could not exist. Through the internet, all the linked hypertext documents available on the web can be accessed.

Berners-Lee at launch of the World Wide Web Foundation.

Over the last decade or so, there has been much discussion in the free world about whether use of the internet should be controlled by the government, and whether its use should be charged for, much like the use of your cell phone. In predictive fashion, Berners-Lee founded the World Wide Web Foundation. Its mission is noted simply as "to advance the open web as a public good and a basic right. It seeks to achieve digital equality — a world where everyone has the same rights and opportunities online."[11]

Whether serendipitously or ironically, the Foundation's headquarters are in Washington D.C. Its work is spread across 70 countries, with 30 employees in three hubs – Jakarta, London, and D.C. In an open letter published in 2018, Berners-Lee implores both those connected to the internet and the yet unconnected 50% of the world to call for action to make it a place accessible by all and to keep the web as "a web worth connecting to."

With WWW now in its 30th year, the Foundation continues its work with "a web worth connecting to" in mind, noting "while the web has created opportunity, given marginalised groups a voice, and made our daily lives easier, it has also created opportunity for scammers, given a voice to those who spread hatred, and made all kinds of crime easier to commit."[12]

At the 2018 web summit held in Lisbon, Spain, Berners-Lee proposed that governments, companies and individual citizens rally together and create a new web contract. The fundamental tenets of that contract would be different for each group, as each group has a different reach and control. His suggestions are as follows.[13]

Governments were asked to agree to three principles:

• Ensure everyone can connect to the internet.

• Avoid any restrictions on internet access, keeping it available to all, all the time.

• Respect the fundamental privacy rights of individuals and protect their data.

Companies were asked to agree to their own set of three principles:

• Make the internet accessible and affordable to everyone.

• Respect and protect people's online personal data and privacy, building online trust.

• Develop technologies that support the best in humanity and challenge the worst.

Citizens were urged to

• Be creators and collaborators on the web.

• Demonstrate a respect for civil discourse and human dignity by building strong communities that support the same principles.

• Fight for the web.

At the 2018 Summit, supporters from all three sectors numbered in the hundreds, all recognizing what TimBL (as he is often referred to) made clear when he said "To achieve the Contract's goals, governments, companies, civil society and individuals must commit to sustained policy development, advocacy, and implementation of the Contract text."[14]

Tim Berners Lee in 2014.

Founder or member of many organizations that support human rights, Berners-Lee was knighted by Queen Elizabeth II in 2004 for his pioneering work. Officially known as Sir Timothy Berners-Lee since then, his credentials include Professorial Fellow at Oxford University, professor at the Massachusetts Institute of Technology (MIT), Director of the World Wide Web Consortium (W3C), holder of the 3Com founders chair at the MIT Computer Science and Artificial Intelligence Laboratory (CSAIL), Director of the Web Science Research Institute (WSRI), MIT advisory board member of the MIT Center for Collective Intelligence, member of the board of trustees of the Ford Foundation, founder and president of the Open Data Institute and a current advisor to the social media and networking service MeWe.

Most people would never have guessed there was so much going on behind the scenes to keep the web open and free, never having heard of many of these organizations. In 2016, TimBL was awarded the Turing Award, named after Alan Turing (mentioned earlier) "for inventing the World Wide Web, the first web browser, and the fundamental protocols and algorithms allowing the Web to scale".[15]

Energy

Climate change and the need to move away from carbon-based technology is driving development in alternative sources of power. In the same way that inexpensive steam power and then electricity propelled advancements in the first industrial revolution, pairing internet with emerging renewable power technology is creating opportunities that began during the third industrial revolution.[16] There is hope that soon, people will be creating and sharing energy sources in a way that is similar to the way we share information on the internet.

Renewable and "green" energy technologies are still developing, but they began to emerge with the other changes that occurred during the third industrial revolution.

Chapter 11: The Fourth Industrial Revolution

– Smaller and Smarter –

Some say that we are now in the Fourth Industrial Revolution. While the third revolution changed computing and the way knowledge is spread, the fourth revolution is purported to mark changes to the digital world on an exponential level. Jeremy Rifkin, in his book The Third Industrial Revolution published in 2011, hinted at this. The term "Fourth Industrial Revolution" was first used by the German economist and engineer Klaus Schwab in a 2015 article published in Foreign Affairs. He is the founder and chairman of the World Economic Forum. The theme of the 2016 annual meeting, held in Davos-Klosters, Switzerland, was "Mastering the Fourth Industrial Revolution." In October of that year, the Forum announced the opening of The

Centre for the Fourth Industrial Revolution in San Francisco, California.

In his book The Fourth Industrial Revolution, Schwab discusses technologies specific to the fourth revolution that combine hardware, software, and biology. Advancements in communication and connectivity will make the application of new technologies easier and more dramatic. Think about the potential in the fields of artificial intelligence (AI), cyber-physical systems like robots, nanotechnology, and quantum computing. The introduction of 5G wireless technologies allows for faster connections to the internet. 3D printing will become commonplace and you will be able to read a book while your car drives you to the grocery store.

Most of these things exist and are in use today, although perhaps not yet readily available. Self-driving cars are out there, but still under development. Nanotechnology is being applied in medicine in the form of tiny robots called nanobots. These are already being tested in humans, and predictions are that by the end of the next decade they will regularly be employed to fight disease and share health information with professionals via "the cloud."

Speaking of which, in computing jargon, the reference to "the cloud" was first coined earlier than many people realize. The term "cloud computing" was first used in a business plan developed by technology execs at Compaq Computer in 1996. They predicted that not only would ALL business transactions eventually be done online, but consumer file storage would eventually move there as well. Now, when people say "the cloud," probably the last thing they think to do is look up to the sky.

Clearly, the fourth industrial revolution will bring about changes that science fiction writers like Ray Bradbury, George Orwell, and Frank Herbert might never have imagined; they would have seemed so far-fetched. Our children will grow up dreaming not of sugarplum fairies, but tiny little robots in their food, perhaps aiding in digestion. When they hear a knock, they won't head for the door but rather reach for their smart phone. Entering their homes of the future, maybe they'll say "Alexa, start the oven, turn on the lights and bring the heat to 70 degrees." (Fahrenheit)

Although sometimes technology can be a curse when it doesn't operate properly, anyone not willing to embrace the rapid changes we see around us will be left behind in ways that will make their lives more difficult as "the good old days" are gone forever.